TO MY NIECE WITH LOVE

INDRAJIT VYAS

Made with ♥ on the Notion Press Platform
www.notionpress.com

To My Dear Niece
Mansi

Contents

CHAPTER ONE

Prologue

31 August 2023

The intention with what I started writing whatever you call this collection of words is something I am not able to resonate with now. So much so that I removed the text I had previously written till this point. Here's what this book was supposed to be about- My life till now.

15 October 2023

It's 11 p.m., usually my sleep time. Today being a Sunday I had no work, and I have yet again wasted another glorious day. I was planning to write today, I wanted to edit a poem and then get back to writing this book. But I ended up doing nothing. The worst part is that most of my week offs are turning out like this.

I started this book about a year ago, I want to finish it by February 2024. I roughly have four months, and I still don't have a clear idea of what I want to write about. Days are rapidly flashing by, and I am not making any progress at all. I can always blame my inability to focus on distractions. While it is true that I prefer a peaceful writing environment, it is still stupid to console myself with excuses. That is like gaslighting or conditioning myself into living an unfulfilled life.

I believe people are like Trees. You must know of bonsai trees. If you don't, they are like miniature trees, made possible by carefully pruning the tree and restricting it to a pot. This makes the tree stop trying to grow to its full size. This is how people keep trees from growing too tall. And this is also how we limit ourselves.

Everyone is capable of achieving everything. But at some point in our lives, we set limiters or we let others set them for us. And that's it, for the rest of our lives, we live with them, never reaching our full potential.

It worked, I wanted to express my displeasure towards myself for not writing as much as I wanted to. You can see the result of that- I ended up writing these many lines. Tomorrow is a day off work too, so hopefully I can write some more.

Now it is time to sleep. I'm not exactly feeling sleepy, but I know if I keep my phone aside and close my eyes, I'll be drifting off to the world of dreams in a jiffy. All my life, I have never had trouble sleeping, (hopefully, it is the same at the time you are reading this book). But a lot of my friends say they have trouble sleeping, I can't exactly relate to them, but I feel that if you listen to your body, your sleep will be set.

I overthink too, I often am thinking while lying on my bed before I doze off. I have dozed off while texting friends, while playing a game on my phone (sucks to find your phone on its last breath the first thing you wake up in the morning), and even while watching stuff. This paragraph shouldn't have existed, I should sleep now.

16 October 2023

Just here to say that today was a repeat of yesterday. Another fabulous day wasted away.

26 October 2023

It has been 10 days since I last touched this project. In this span, I had three continuous holidays. By now it should be understandable how those days were spent.

I have an idea of what to write about, I have had it for a long time now. But before I go about with it, I'd like to explain what this book was supposed to be about, and the original intention behind it.

Long story short- I was extremely disappointed and annoyed with my father for forcing me to take up a different stream of education from the one I wanted to pursue. All this because of peer pressure, which I felt was stupid, I still feel it is stupid, but anyway, you get the point right?

I should thank my lazy self for not proceeding on that path because the resulting book would be a rant against the world. I doubt anyone would find pleasure in reading that, I wouldn't.

So instead I thought I would write something like a guide, a collection of my experiences and what I learned from them till now. I don't know who this will benefit, or if this even benefits anyone at all. I won't concern myself with that because here's why I'm writing this- I believe we have more to learn from people's failures than their successes. The paths to success are few, but on the other hand, countless paths lead to failure. Instead of trying them all out, you could avoid the missteps others took, and proceed in the right direction.

Earlier I said I wanted to finish this book by February 2024, the reason behind that deadline is your birthday. For your first birthday, I wanted to give you something valuable. After some pondering, this is what I came up with. I was hoping I could give you something to draw parallels with, a reference material to help you develop something of your own.

Obviously, you can't read it now, you can't even speak yet. But someday you could read this, maybe you are reading it now.

27 October 2023

There are plenty of what-ifs involved with this book, will you ever read it, if yes, then when? But that's like placing the cart before the horse because I'm not even sure if you will have a reading habit in the first place. But your Dad and Mom both used to read, they still do perhaps. So I'm hoping you catch that habit too. And then there's the question of other people, will they want to read this? Will they like it? Will I even complete this? If I do, will I manage to publish this?

I don't have answers to any of these questions, I don't need them either because I know time will tell me. But if you are reading this, you will certainly know the answers to at least a few of these questions.

Before I start writing about everything that I can think of, here's a disclaimer of sorts- Everything I'll be writing about is my experiences, opinions, and interpretation of life. Everything is from my perspective, so expect everything to be biased. Nothing here is meant to change you or teach you how to live your life. Use whatever you find here however you please, just don't think of this as me trying to push some ideas into your head. With that said, it is time to start this for real.

I don't know when you might read this, so I'm having trouble deciding where and what to start with. I guess I'll start from the beginning, I'll take you back as far as my memories allow me to.

3 Nov 2023

It has exactly been a week since I last worked on this project, if I am to complete this in time, I will most likely have to write every day for the next couple of months. There's editing, proofreading, and other publishing-related work to be researched and carried out too.

I know it looks pretty bleak, but my choices are simple and binary- Write, or continue to wallow in a world of excuses and delusional self-indulgence. Truthfully speaking, the latter is easier-living a reactive life, floating in a polluted river like a piece of trash, going wherever the currents carry me.

But living this life is as unsettling as it is easy, and it makes me go all queasy. Every night when I lie down to sleep, I drift further away from my dreams than I was yesterday. Then I wake up in the morning to repeat the routine of the previous day, and in the night I fall asleep not wanting to dream.

Throughout this entire process of self-ruination, the worst part is being aware of the path I'm walking, the place it will lead me to, and yet... continuing on it. I see myself turning into a pathetic shadow of what I could have been, slowly melding into the darkness, like heavy clouds in a stormy sky that disappears after a single night's shower.

Will this go on forever on a loop? Till the record is so hopelessly scratched that it screeches instead of playing a song? It surely will, if I don't break away. I only see one way out of this- by writing. Writing away from this self-prophesied path of doom.

I'm ending this here today, but I'll be back tomorrow, to write again.

4 Nov 2023

Surprisingly, I returned.

I identified the major bottlenecks that were hindering my ability to write consistently. Discounting household distractions, what I'm left with are my cravings to finish the anime on my watchlist, and writing. Yeah, you read that right- "writing."

This isn't the only thing I was writing, I was writing articles for my medium blog once in a while, editing my old poems to post on social media, and writing new poems whenever I chanced upon an idea. But now I have decided to abstain from further creative endeavors till I finish this, the only exception to this rule being poems. Because I randomly find ideas for them, and it doesn't happen too often. (I am basically betting on my inconsistency here).

That was all about optimizing my available writing time. The next step is increasing my writing window. I travel five days a week to my office by public transport, this traveling time is nowhere near insignificant. I read or listen to music throughout this everyday road trip. But yesterday, I wrote most of what you read on my phone. Even now as you are reading this, I'm doing the exact same thing as yesterday- sitting beside an open window, feeling the cool wind (slightly polluted) on my face, and flanked by strangers hooked to their phones, I'm typing out my thoughts on a 6.5-inch mobile device.

Now I ask myself, why didn't I start doing this any sooner? I already know the answer, you may too.

It was never about time and never will be. I always had time, we all do. It's about how we use it, it's about priorities, it's about you.

Speaking of time, it's about time I get to the point furthest away from where I am, ...no, from when I am.

I'm sitting in a dark corner with utensils strewn all around me. Now don't go around imagining the worst, I was just playing with utensils in my grandmother's kitchen. I can't exactly remember if this was before I was in kindergarten or while in it. But it's from when I was 2 or 3 years old. I vaguely remember spending a lot of my pre-kindergarten days here.

The reason- my sister, she's a year younger than me, so when my mom had her, my aunt aka her sister helped ease her burden by caring for me. So I ended up being raised by her at my grandparents' home. Hence that kitchen anecdote.

And now all of a sudden, something struck me, I wasn't playing with those utensils in that kitchen. I was hiding there with them hoping I would be camouflaged by them.

It's weird how our brains work, moments ago when I tried to recall one of my oldest memories, I only managed to recall it partially, and before I fully became aware of that fact, my brain filled that incomplete memory and fed it to me, sort of like an autofill feature on a smartphone.

As soon as I had written down that false memory, the real one surfaced.

What was I doing there hiding? Who was I hiding from? Did I commit some mischief? Or was someone out there to get me? Once I narrate what actually transpired, the answer is quite unsurprisingly simple.

Growing up with my aunt, I had grown quite attached to her, so whenever my dad came by to take me to my actual home, I would run away, dive under chairs, hide behind utensils, and do anything that kept me away from his arm's reach.

But eventually, I had to go home, because it was time to get me started with my education, or should I say- institutionalization.

5 Nov 2023

I have always been fascinated by the human mind and the limitless potential it holds. When you are trying to piece together fragments of old memories, the restored memory might not exactly be intact. It is like looking at an old photograph and trying to recall the memory associated with it, your brain uses whatever bits of information it has stored and guesses the rest. This is how people form false memories, and this is also how false memories can be planted in other people.

When a person remembers just some bits of information about a particular incident, any information they get from other parties either consciously or subconsciously about that particular incident forms a basis on which their brain builds their memory. This brings to the table the question of reliability, how sure can you be of yourself?

The human brain employs many mechanisms to make processing information easier, it uses shortcuts called heuristics to help make decisions faster. This isn't necessarily bad, but the tradeoff for speed here is reliability.

In addition to features like these, there are so many other safety mechanisms built into our brains, that there is simply too much to discuss, if I continued on this matter I suspect this book would get filled with random bits of abstract information about the human brain. This is after all a subject as deep as the universe, if not more.

6 Nov 2023

It is just past 10 PM and it has been raining for quite some time, it is unimaginably calm compared to the distracting day. I put into order what I had written yesterday, and it is time to start today's ritual.

Yesterday I was talking about memories, while I would love to continue further with that subject, I assure you it would be best if I do not. Why, you ask? Because firstly, I'm no expert on that subject, whatever I might have said may not be true either, all of that was based on my understanding, so I suggest you do your own research if you are interested in that topic. Secondly, there are plenty of other subjects to explore, so if I stay at this station too long, my train of thought is certain to get derailed.

But before I switch, here's a question for you-

What are memories? A recollection of your past? Moments you have lost? Are they something to remember? Or are they something, because you remembered?

I last ended my tale taking a dig at education. Don't get the wrong notion about me hating education, I have nothing against it. I have nothing against an education system that readies you for the world by teaching things of value. But, was the education system I was part of, like that? No.

Instead of teaching students how to fish, they are (or were) teaching them how to calculate interest for the loans they will be applying to buy that said fish. Not a tasteful analogy (especially for vegans), I know, but it is what it is.

I still can't seem to find uses for the hundreds of math formulae I had to learn, and I don't want another brainwashed idiot (sorry, I couldn't think of a milder word) to try to tell me otherwise, when they are struggling hard to convince themselves that the time they spent studying all that wasn't in vain.

Those formulae aren't useless, but tell me what use does Ariel have for a matchbox in her underwater palace? What use does a bald man have for a comb? A comb and a matchbox, neither of them are useless, they are useful in the right places, but most certainly not in every situation.

At the time of you reading this, if you are still in school or college, don't let all my talk about education get to you. Demotivating you is the last thing I want to do. The education system I'm speaking of is from decades ago, so I don't think it will be the same wherever and whenever you are studying (I sincerely hope it is not).

7 Nov 2023

There is this fox story I remember reading in someone's school textbook. It is about a fox that tries to reach for grapes high up a wall. It tries and tries, but it cannot reach it, in the end, it gives up and comforts itself by saying that the grapes are sour.

Now why am I randomly narrating a fable of a fox and grapes? Because I want to establish something concretely- I am that fox, but I have tasted those grapes and they were indeed sour, but I can't say the same for that fox in the story. It is sort of like Schrodinger's cat (if you don't know of it, please look it up, it's very interesting).

During my school time, I got good grades, was almost a model student, and was a certified teacher's pet. So don't write me off as some sore loser getting back at the education system because he sucked at school.

I was recently arranging the certificates I had obtained for participating in and winning competitions during my school time. The first one I had acquired was during kindergarten, it was for getting first place in a drawing contest. I don't remember what I drew then, but I can assure you that I'm no artist.

I used to draw mustaches on unsuspecting poets and bestow hair on balding authors in my English and other language textbooks. During the last phase of my education, I doodled in my notebooks to keep me from falling prey to the lecturers' deathly effective lullabies. This is also when I started writing poems as an alternate strategy to beat boredom.

Anyways, kindergarten was for two years, probably when I was 3-4 years old or 4-5. I can't remember much of it other than being sent to neighboring classrooms to fetch dusters and canes. I also learned a valuable lesson which I appreciate to this day. I coughed on my teacher without covering my mouth, she made me stand in a corner for the rest of the class to teach me some manners, I bet she would be happy to know that it worked spectacularly. I have been a changed man, or should I say changed kid since then. I took measures to not inconvenience people as much as possible. Now whenever I see people (fully grown adults, not kids) openly sneezing, coughing, and spitting in public places, I pity them for not having someone to teach them basic manners.

8 Nov 2023

My mom started working as a teacher (at a different school) in my second year of kindergarten, so every day I and my sister waited for our mom to come and walk us home after classes were done.

It was during these waits that I developed an interest in the field of martial arts. After school hours, older students had karate training classes on the school grounds. Idly waiting to return home, I used to watch them practice their karate moves. I hazily remember being a part of that practicing group for a short duration, but I don't remember how or when. This, in addition to watching action movies further increased my passion for all things martial arts.

Spoiler alert: I have never to this day (at the time of writing this book) learned any form of martial arts. The most I did was read a book on Jiu-Jitsu and Judo and watch some martial arts movies.

I could have at least learned one form of martial arts. I asked my parents a couple of times when I was around ten, but they didn't make much of an effort to find a training institute, and I did not persist any further. As time flew by, the amount of resources accessible at my fingertips only grew. I had to think and I'd be, but I was neither focused nor self-disciplined enough to make the most of what was available to me.

9 Nov 2023

Martial arts is all about discipline, and focus, and determination, and ...a lot of other things. The thing is, it instills a great amount of discipline in its practitioners, and it also demands an equal amount of discipline from the people seeking to pursue it.

I just sat down at my bus stop, I heard a shout some distance away. I turn around and what do I see? A middle-aged man stripped down to his underwear chasing after a dog, hurling curses at it. This is like a moment straight out of a cartoon, life is so random.

Continuing on, martial arts serve as a constant reminder of what our bodies are capable of, what our minds are capable of, and what we are capable of.

Why would you want a weapon when you could turn yourself into one?

10 Nov 2023

To the eyes of the uncouth, martial arts is violent, it is the way of the brutes, it is something that merely gives you an edge when in a fight.

I just witnessed a car bump into a car in front of it, and that in turn bumped into another car, this is on a major high-traffic road. Now if these cars stop in the middle of the road (they will) and start arguing... I pray for the commuters behind them.

Like I said before- life is so random.

Well, if you interpret martial arts that way, you couldn't be any more wrong. I'll interrupt the flow again to tell you that there are many deadly martial arts or derivatives of them that were specifically developed to kill and cause grievous injury. Krav Maga is one such example.

Martial arts were originally meant for self-defense, and the best defense is a good offense. You can pretty much sum up martial arts with that. But let's not end it with that.

A true martial artist is not just physically fit and strong, their mental strength is immense. They have a great understanding of human physiology and psychology, in addition to various other concepts of science. They read people at a glance, they know where and when to strike. They know how to deliver the maximum impact with the least possible force. Their movements are fluid and minimal, a performance more than a fight, a sublime dance to behold.

Similarly in life, every role is multi-faceted and layered, don't straightaway dismiss anything as simple, there's always more to what meets the eye.

11 Nov 2023

I feel I am not writing as much as I should be, with the current pacing I doubt I could complete this book. Weekends are key, I better not squander them like I usually do.

Yesterday I talked about not taking things at face value, while that is true, the inverse of that is just as true.

I strongly believe that Life is the personification of infinite irony. Everything I talk about in this book, and this book itself serves to emphasize my statement.

The simplest of things are the most complex to understand, and vice versa.

Other than that martial arts episode, I hardly remember much about those days. I have faint recollections of listening to the FM radio before leaving for school.

I'll interrupt again to sneak in an incident from my present. A lady in her 30s carrying a small child climbed aboard the bus at the previous stop and started begging. She was handing passengers a piece of paper with something printed on it. I didn't accept it, but I can tell you with a 98% surety what was printed on it. Either her child or her husband has a severe health condition, and their family can't afford the medical procedure to help them. That is why she's looking for donations from random people.

You can call me a bad person for ignoring her, I don't mind in the slightest, because the directions in my moral compass do not align with yours. That said, I have given to people who have come to me asking, at times I have given when I wasn't even asked.

So why give then, why not now? I felt like giving then, I didn't feel the same way now. It is as simple as that. I had money in my wallet, giving her ten rupees wouldn't make a difference to me in the slightest, but it would have made at least a slight difference to her if her cause was real, if it wasn't, well she's one depraved wretch.

When I said ten rupees wouldn't have made the slightest difference to me, I made an overstatement. In actuality, it does. I don't earn lakhs of rupees a month, what I earn is a basic salary, lower than what most of my friends earn. But the silver lining here is that I like what I'm doing, and my friends can't exactly say the same about their jobs.

I can switch to a different company and earn more, I now have the base experience that is required. But it feels pointless to switch just for that. I need money, I don't want it.

Every time I see a beggar (which is a lot) I have the urge to give to them. It's not because I want to farm good karma or reserve my place in heaven, that is the last thing I care for. It is the act itself that matters to me, if I had the power to change someone's situation, I would do it. For me, it could be next to nothing or something at most, but for them, that could change everything.

Now if I started giving to every beggar I came across, I would sooner or later join their troupe, trailing strangers for pocket change, like dogs do their owners for treats.

I learned only a couple of years ago the concept of "Noblesse Oblige." I liked it, It loosely says that those with power and privilege should try to help the less privileged.

When I was younger, I always thought that if or when I got rich someday, I would help the poor. But aren't the rich people rich because they don't help the poor?

That said, I believe we don't have the right to tell others what to do with their money unless it is your money, but if it was your money it wouldn't be theirs. They earned it through whatever means they employed, so it is up to them to do whatever they want with it. Cursing them for not parting with their wealth is plain jealousy, instead of wanting them to do charity, why don't you get rich and practice what you are preaching instead? Now it's not so easy, isn't it?

To judge someone's action is easy, the cause behind it? Not so much.

16 Nov 2023

4 days, I thought I'd be gone longer. Right after I said weekends are key, I started reading manhwa again, that is how I spent these last four days.

Manhwa are Korean comics of sorts, I have read a decent amount of them before. Reading them is like entering an ever-expanding rabbit hole. You finish one, you find another, and then another, and so on till you get tired of them or find something else that distracts you from them.

So I estimated I would be jumping around from one manhwa to another for a minimum of a week to a maximum of two. I completed reading one, started another, finished it, and picked out five more to read next. But at that point, I felt this book calling out to me. Maybe it was my subconscious memory tugging at my conscious self, armed with the knowledge that my aunt would have brought you back to India by this time next month. Your parents are supposed to join you the month after that. Soon after that is your birthday month, my deadline.

I knew all of this, but I still went ahead and did what I did. Why? Because it made me happy? I wouldn't call this happy. Happiness is something very different from what this gave me. It entertained me, I enjoyed it. That is not what happiness is, at least to me it is not. Because the time I spent enjoying here came at a cost. I exchanged a part of my future- a possibility of my future, for this present, now my past.

All the time you have now is borrowed from your future, and everything that you spend belongs to your past. The present has no time to call its own, it exists outside the bounds of time.

This might not make much sense, but it is understandable to not be able to understand the indefinite, especially when it is outside the planes of existence.

Throughout your life you will encounter countless nonsensical things, or should I say concepts that you won't understand. Exploring them, or trying to explore them makes life interesting. Take this book for example, it is just me trying to have a one-sided conversation with you crossing the boundaries of time.

Now that I have wasted some time talking about time, let's go back in time.

After finishing kindergarten, we sold our home and moved to a new neighborhood. This was sort of an underdeveloped area, so we got to buy double the land we previously had plus get a small house constructed in it with the money we made by selling our old home.

Houses aren't built in a day, so we stayed in a rented house while we waited for the construction to be complete. It was a new house and a new school for me.

Before continuing further I'll tell you how the basic education process in my time was split. It may or may not be the same here now, but just in case it changes, or if you study in the US or some other country, this bit of information will help you understand things more clearly.

Formal education starts with Kindergarten which is for two years. Year one is called Lower Kindergarten or LKG. Year two is Upper Kindergarten or UKG. Next, we move to what we call The School. Depending on what regulatory board the school is affiliated with, it can last for 10 or 12 years, consisting of 10 or 12 grades respectively.

The school I studied in was under the state regulatory board for the first year, then it converted to the central board. But it still only had 10 grades, after completing the 10th grade we could join a different school under the central board and continue with 11th and 12 grade, or we could start college with other students from the state board.

What we call college is Pre-University College or PUC, it is a course for two years. Those studying grade 11 and 12 don't have to complete this, since both the courses are supposed to be equivalent. The third choice is a Diploma course, which is for three years. That is the one your dad chose.

After completing any of these three, you could proceed with the Bachelor's degree or some other course, each with a different duration. If you want to study further there are Master's degrees, doctorates, and other things which I can't be bothered to remember. But I'd like to tell you that your Dad did his Master's degree after finishing up with a Bachelor's course in Engineering.

I won't elaborate on any of this again, so make a note or keep a bookmark here so you can come back and make sense of what I'll be referring to in later parts.

17 Nov 2023

During my kindergarten, school, college, and even now after I have started working, there has been one constant throughout the years- me looking forward to holidays. I never understood my friends who wanted the vacations to end quickly so they could come back to school/college. I don't get them to this day.

We didn't have much in terms of entertainment at my home, so during kindergarten whenever we got long holidays I used to pester my mom to take me to my grandmother's home. I would spend the entirety of my holidays there. We went there on most Sundays too.

Unlike at my home, my grandparents had a television set with a multitude of channels. My grandfather watched the news early morning, astrology followed next, and then movies throughout the day. In the evening my aunt and grandmother watched soap operas. I sometimes watched movies with my grandfather, but I was always on the prowl, waiting and watching for gaps in this busy TV-watching schedule. And gaps I did find- early morning before the news anchors began babbling, and whenever my grandfather went out for a stroll or took a daytime nap.

Take away the television and I had my cousin. We played board games, we used to fight (the last one was sometime during kindergarten) and the moment he so much as touched me, I'd run to my aunt to complain.

There's this guy sitting right beside me now, rambling on and on, on his phone ever since he boarded the bus. He has stopped now, but the damage is done, he managed to distract me for a moment. All these days I was able to write while traveling on the bus not because it was empty and noiseless. It was because of the exact opposite reason.

The buses I have to take are overcrowded, the seats are rarely available, and you could consider yourself lucky if you manage to get standing space. Expecting a peaceful environment in such scenarios is akin to finding cost-effective and decent food portions in fancy fine-dining restaurants.

So what's the trick you ask? Almost every time, the people trying to pull you down end up being your stepping stones. Inside the bus I have around 80 odd people chattering, generating noises in all ways possible, and outside I have hundreds of vehicles- suspension creaking, tires screeching, engines roaring, with their senseless drivers' frustratedly honking. All these noises combine, forming a shield keeping me from tuning in on any one single noise source, unless I consciously want to. But earlier, things were silent for once and the guy next to me was the sole source of disruption. Unless I am in the flow state, there is little chance of me not getting distracted from that. This is also one of the major issues that I face at my home, everything is silent except for that one random person in my family generating noise.

Anyway, that was how I spent my vacations till grade 4 in school. But before I could go to my grandparents' place to start enjoying my vacation there was something important I had to address- Homework. The moment we got an extra holiday, the teachers were ready to pile us with work to keep us busy during the holidays. So to counter this tasteless evil scheme of theirs, on the last day of school i.e. the day before the holidays begin, I used to rush home and start with my homework. That day and the next were what I needed to finish all, if not most of the assigned homework.

My friends and even my teachers have this wrong impression of me, they think I'm studious because I finish and submit my homework, and assignments on time. They weren't even close, I finished them as soon as possible because they were a hassle, an eyesore. They were the most horrendous of the leeches, sucking away my free time for almost no good purpose! I wanted to be rid of them immediately, end of story. It was something I had to do, not what I wanted to do.

In the first grade I was immature (I still am), I craved attention, and I wanted to win. This phase lasted till grade 3. During this time, I was my class topper straight for two years, and the go-to class monitor too. In grade 1, I still remember slipping and falling purposefully in the classroom to attract attention. I used to race my friends on who would copy down the things written on the blackboard onto our notebooks first. I participated in running races and lost hopelessly. I did what kids do.

In grade 2 I did something stupid, and my teacher did the perfect thing to make me realize my mistake. We had class tests throughout my school and even college life. So back in grade 2, there was this English test. It was for 25 marks, only I and another kid scored 24, and that was the highest score. I alone wanted the highest score, and just one mark stood between me and that perfect score. That peak of absolute supremacy was inches away from my foot.

What I did next was sneak under the bench with a pencil, an eraser, and that notebook in which I took the test. In less than a minute, I was walking to the teacher with my test notebook, I told her there was a counting mistake and got that one mark that rightfully belonged to me. I proudly came back and took my seat, the perfect crime... but alas, If only things went as planned.

A girl was sitting on the same bench as me, she had to go tell the teacher of the grave and unforgivable sin that I committed. My teacher looked at me, I still remember the look of her eyes from that day- they weren't angry, they weren't pitying, they weren't disgusted. They were calm like the all-encompassing sea, floating on their surface was a single question- Why?

I had no answer to give her other than my shameful silence. She didn't change my test score back to 24, I had obtained that one extra mark but at what cost? She didn't punish or reprimand me, she asked me to tell my mom that she wanted to speak to her. I was scared, not because my mom would scold me, but because I had brought shame to her and her upbringing by committing this despicable act.

After school, I told my mom that my English teacher wanted to meet her, she asked me why, and I lied saying I didn't know. While on the way to school with my mom I saw that girl again, she was pointing at me mouthing the words- "Cheater! Cheater!"

My mom inquired with me about it, I denied not knowing anything again. Soon after that, my teacher met with my mom, they conversed for a while. On the way home, I knew for certain that my teacher hadn't said a single word about what had happened earlier that day. My mom didn't tell me anything about the chat she just had, neither did I ask, but I knew they talked about some other unrelated matter. Don't ask me how I know, I just do.

That was the first and last time I cheated in tests.

Back then I didn't have an answer to my teacher's question, but slowly over the next few years, I learned it.

My teacher knew fully well that I was capable of acing that test, I knew that too. Then why?

Greed.

18 November 2023

My teacher knew I was better than that, and she conveyed that to me without ever uttering a single word, her lesson to me was subtle, but it was one of the most valuable lessons that I had learned.

Why did I do it?

I wanted to stand above them all, just standing at the peak wasn't enough, I wanted to fly higher.

Later I thought about that test and those marks, what were they for?

I was trying to get some writing done before I left for work, but it was noisy at home. So I decided to leave for the bus stop early, it's at least peaceful there. Now I have around 50 to 70 minutes till my bus' usual arrival time, plenty of time to write.

I soon found an answer, those marks were to assess my knowledge, to test how much I knew. They weren't there to proclaim to my classmates that I was better than them. They weren't there to prove to the teachers that I was the best student there was, or to my parents that I was studying well and their hard-earned money was being put to good use.

From that moment onwards, I didn't try to prove anything to anyone unless it was necessary or I gained something out of it.

This overly competitive spirit I had was partly inherent, partly due to it being a characteristic trait of that immature age, but it was mostly due to my father.

He always wanted me and my sister to get the first rank in everything, second place was worthless. Once you did get first place, not getting the perfect score was a crime. There was no satisfying him, the result day after the final examinations every year was nerve-racking. It always ended with a flurry of scoldings, beatings, and the most asked question- Why we couldn't be better than whoever was the first ranker? This story is commonplace in most Indian households.

I didn't care about any of this, but I was weary of the result day. If anything, I needed incentives to perform, so in grade 2 my dad promised to buy me a Train set if I secured the first rank. I did, but the promise wasn't kept. Unfortunately for him and me, I held grudges and I was unpredictably petty. Since then I didn't ever try to get rank 1 in my class, nor did I trust anyone to keep their promises.

Boredom can drive you to do weird things. When I was at home during the holidays, boredom was my constant companion. The textbooks for the next grade were always issued during the long holidays after the final examinations. These holidays lasted roughly two months, by now you should know how and where I spent the majority of them. The remainder of these days were boring.

To counter boredom, I started reading textbooks. At first, it was the English textbook and then the language books, because these always had stories in them. Once I was done with these, I read every other textbook I had, other than the maths book. Thus developed my reading habit. It was a habit born of boredom.

In those days my mom held tuition classes in our home. Students from various grades and schools would come to be tutored. This was the perfect opportunity for me, I borrowed their English textbooks and started reading the stories in them.

Starting from grade 3, we were allowed into our school library, but it was only once a week and for just 45 minutes. If some teacher was lagging in completing their syllabus, we would have to say goodbye to the library. I used to wait for this library period every week, we weren't allowed to pick books, but I liked reading whatever was given to me.

By this time I had zero interest in getting rank 1 or proving anything to anyone. Reading plus all the previous incidents opened me to a whole new perspective. I wasn't running the same race as everyone else anymore. Funnily enough, I stopped participating in running races and other sports competitions, because I wasn't physically capable enough, I knew it was a pointless venture which would only waste my energy.

I didn't study much either, the only time I did study was on the day of the tests or examinations. I paid attention during classes and skimmed through the books on the exam mornings, I continued this tradition throughout my educational life. This practice kept my rank hovering between 2 and 3 throughout my school years. I didn't drop down a rank below that nor did I go above it. I was at perfect equilibrium.

In grade 3 a new girl joined our class, her name was Anushka. She said she was from Solapur, Maharashtra. She had to move here with her family due to her dad being transferred here, If my memory serves me right, that's what she said.

All the boys in our class were out to impress her, I was somehow part of that group too. Unfortunately for the other boys, our Kannada teacher made her sit beside me. She wanted me to help the new girl with the Kannada language as she was alien to it. And help I did, within half a year not only did she learn it, but she also scored more than me in that language tests. I didn't feel the slightest tinge of jealousy, instead, I was impressed by her learning ability, and though it's silly, I felt a bit proud of my tutelage too. She was a very talented kid, she was good at studies, and sports and could even perform Bharatanatyam like a professional dancer. I and two other friends had formed a friend circle, she quickly became part of that group. We all played and ate lunch together, those days were blissful. But like how all good things come to an end, this story had to end too, albeit incompletely.

That year flew by quickly, on the result day when we had to go with our parents to get our progress card, I and my friends learned that she was leaving the school. Her father had gotten transferred again. That was the last we saw or heard of her. If she had stayed, I'm pretty sure I would be hovering between rank 3 and 4 instead of 2 and 3.

This was also the last time I tried to impress anyone. It wasn't because I was heartbroken, crushed, or anything along those lines. I just learned that I didn't need to. While I was initially trying to impress her, I quickly realized it was a stupid thing to do. I genuinely wanted to help her, and I didn't jump at every opportunity I got to show off to her. Because of this, we became friends quickly, even though it was only for a short while.

I don't remember anything significant or life-changing happening in grade 4. I was my usual self, I wasn't seeking attention anymore, I read what books I got from the students attending my mom's tuition classes, and whatever my school librarian deemed fit for us to read.

Now I remember an incident, in the holidays after writing the final examination of grade 4, I went to my father's hometown with my parents. We stayed there for a few days, and when it was time for us to leave, my family left me behind and went back home. Before leaving, my father told his cousin to teach me swimming. I didn't want to stay there, much less learn to swim.

After a few reluctant days, I got used to that place. One fine day it was time to begin my swimming lessons, it was a very unexpected lesson. My uncle tied a plastic can to my back and pushed me into a huge well, the water in that well was two stories below ground level, I estimated it to be around 20 feet. Although people were swimming in the well when I was pushed into it, it gave me quite a fright. As soon as I floated back up, I latched onto an old man who was swimming nearby. He swam me to the side of the well where the stairs were located. I quickly climbed out, put on my clothes, and dashed to my temporary place of residence. That swimming lesson made me not take any other future swimming lessons.

Later on, my uncle told me that kids half my age could dive into that well and swim like fish could. So what? I couldn't care less if infants could swim down to the Mariana Trench. I was a sheltered city-dwelling kid, this is not how you teach us to swim, this is how you give lasting traumas for life.

It's the same with subjects in school too, no subject sucks, it's the way they are taught that changes everything. Teach them in an easy-to-understand manner, and it is suddenly everyone's favorite subject. Do the opposite, and unsurprisingly, the students will hate that subject for life.

After spending almost a month there, I returned home, I don't remember how though, I must have tagged back with some relative. Although I had a decently good time back at that place, I still thought it would have been a lot nicer if I had spent that whole time at my grandparents' place instead.

20 November 2023

Yesterday I didn't do much, I woke up and started waiting for the cricket match to start. It was the World Cup finals between India and Australia, unfortunately for us, India lost. A very disheartening day, I wasn't into cricket much till a couple of years ago. My friends always used to discuss it and I got dragged into the gentleman's game. Now I wish I wasn't.

This loss was very upsetting because India won every other match in this World Cup overwhelmingly. They played and they lost, but it doesn't end there, now start the actual games- Players getting blamed and badmouthed for losing the match. If that wasn't enough, there are some idiots attacking Australian players, abusing them on their social media. Why curse them? They won fair and square, accept our loss, and let them be. And for those cursing our players through their TV, phone, and computer screens, why don't you go out there and play instead? What, Do your knees hurt? Can't run 100 meters without gasping for air?

There is a reason why they are on the pitch out there, while you are sitting on your hindquarters watching them. If you are better than them, go out on the field and prove it, get us a trophy, if you can't, then please pack your piehole with whatever junk you can find.

Imagine how the players would be feeling, they would be beating themselves up more than any spectator would dare abuse them.

What's done is done, we learn from it and move ahead wiser than we were before. Here's the single most important thing that I have learned from everything in life: Every situation you encounter, you can categorize into one of these two- those that you can change, and those you cannot. If you learn to accurately do that, you will be in control of your life.

Nothing is impossible to change, but the effort involved could be very steep, not to mention the impact it could have on you. This is what I mean when I say "situations you cannot change."

Now you encounter an unfavorable situation, you don't like it, what can you do about it? Can you change it? If yes, do it. If not, ignore it and move on. It is pointless to waste your time and energy on doing anything else other than changing it.

That was too simple, things are not always that simple. there's more to the black-and-white binary choices. So here's another one. You are in high school, there is a silent girl in your class who is always being bullied by another girl and her friends. The bullied girl won't tell the teacher, you don't know why. You have watched this happen far too many times, you can't keep watching this happen throughout the school term, your conscience won't allow you to. What will you do?

You can secretly inform the teacher, but then the bullies might think the girl they bullied complained against them and start bullying her harder. If by some chance they find out that you ratted them out, they might start targeting you too. Are you capable of facing them if they decide to do that?

You could directly tell the bullies off, but do you have the courage to do that, and then deal with the repercussions?

You could speak to the bullied girl, motivate her, and make her stand up for herself. But that could also make the situation worse than before for her.

You could befriend and convince the bullies that the girl they bully is not worth the effort. You could distract them with something else, you could slowly make them turn over a new leaf.

If you want to change the situation there are so many choices to pick from, each leading to a newer albeit stranger situation, what will you do? If you don't want the hassle of making a choice and dealing with the aftermath then you could choose to do nothing, ignoring the entire thing altogether. This means you are accepting that you cannot change the situation. This is how everything is, while technically you can change the "unchangeable situations", you choose not to because of causality.

You either help the bullied girl or you don't, the choices don't matter as long as you choose something. Because you have either used your energy to achieve an outcome or conserved it to prevent another.

Here's another choice- it's more of a state than a choice, I call it the "Cat on a wall state." While in this state you are worrying about that girl, feeling sorry for her, feeling helpless, feeling powerless, and you do a lot of other passive things.

You neither helped her nor ignored her. This is the worst state to be in if you want to be in control. Because you are pointlessly wasting your time and energy every millisecond you spend in this state.

There's a quote by Dante that I like-

> "*The darkest places in hell are reserved for those who maintain their neutrality in times of moral crisis.*"

None of what I said was about morality, this was all about control and causality.

21 November 2023

Three days ago I remembered another incident, I wasn't exactly sure if it happened during grade 3 or 4. I asked my mom, and she wasn't sure either, I then called my aunt aka your grandmother. She has an excellent memory, I only had to tell her of the incident, and she gave me the day, date, and year of when it happened. She would have even told me the time if I had asked for it.

This happened when I was in grade 3, on September 15th, 2007. It was on Ganesha Chaturthi. The previous night we received word that a relative of ours had died. To attend her funeral my grandparents, their children, and their families aka Your Grandmother and father, My mom and our family, an uncle of mine, and two other relatives left early on the morning of the 15th on a minibus (a 20 seater bus).

On the way to the funeral, the bus we were in suddenly made a screeching noise and veered off the highway, racing towards a steep fall. I only noticed when the bus violently jerked and sent me flying forward along with everyone else on the bus. The bus had hit a small rock and come to a halt. If not for the rock, we would have directly met the relative whose funeral we had set out to attend. Because that rock was just at the end of the hill, and it was the only thing keeping the bus from crashing down the hill into the boulders down below.

We got off the bus, walked a little distance from it, and tried to process what had just happened. Fortunately, no one was hurt except a relative whose bangles had broken and scratched her wrist. The bus too was almost intact, other than a bent front bumper. A bunch of locals gathered around to check on us. They said we were very lucky to have escaped alive, much less without any injuries. That spot was said to be an accident-prone zone that had sent a lot of lives packing to the afterlife. They even showed us the debris of an SUV that had crashed there last week, unfortunately for them, they weren't as lucky as us and had instantly died on the spot.

We got a mechanic, fixed the bus, and were back on our way in a couple of hours. We attended the funeral and came back home on that same bus safely.

Although it was a major incident that could have changed my life completely or snuffed it out, it had little to no impact on me. It was probably due to my age back then, I might not have understood the full scope of things.

Whoever said "Ignorance is Bliss," was right on the money. The lesser you know the more peaceful you can be.

22 November 2023

I was tired and sleepy yesterday, couldn't write as much as I wanted to.

Grade 5 is when I moved on to the next phase of my life. Previously, I had stopped trying to gain attention, but from here onwards I started trying actively to not attract any attention toward me. Books were mostly responsible for that.

In our English textbook in grade 5, there was an excerpt from a novel. It was from "Around the World in 80 Days," the moment I read it, I wanted to know more. I checked in grade 6's English textbook to see if there would be a continuation of it to be found there. I found nothing. My mom told me to check with her brother the next time we went to my grandmother's home. I did just that, and he had that book, along with so many other classics. All these were abridged versions, perfect for me to read. It was initially hard to read them, there were no pictures and there were hundreds of pages of text. My curiosity was the only thing keeping me going, and finally, it led me to finish that book. I spent the entirety of the holidays reading those books after finishing grade 5.

In grade 5 the school library restrictions were lifted, but not as much as I would have liked, but it was much better compared to the previous years.

Every day of school from Monday to Friday was divided into 7-8 periods, this was excluding the lunch break. Saturdays were half days, hence we had 4 periods on those days.

In grade 5 we had two library periods a week. While we now could pick whatever book we wanted to read, we also could get a library card and borrow books. I made full use of these newfound privileges. I read whatever I could in the library and borrowed a book to read at home. I would aim to finish it before the next library period so I could borrow a different book. Initially, the librarian was very skeptical when I went to return a book just two days after borrowing it. After signing in the book register a few more times, she got used to it. By the end of grade 7, I finished reading all the English books in the fiction section of our library. Then I read a couple of Kannada books, and after that, I read whatever random book I could find.

The library periods could get canceled if the librarian went on a leave, or if some other teacher decided to hijack this period to complete their syllabus. Towards the end of the academic year, when the exams were close by, the library periods were canceled altogether. Starting from grade 8 we didn't have any library periods, that was the last I read anything from my school library.

After finishing my uncle's collection, and my school library, I had no more books to read in grade 7. That was when I started spending the entirety of the money I had saved up, on books.

I didn't want attention because it came at the cost of time, and I wanted every second I could spare, to read, and to dive into the multi-faceted and wondrous worlds of words.

All this reading was creatively and intellectually stimulating. Even though I mostly read fiction, I learned a lot from those books. Every book took me to a brand new world, immersing me completely in them. All the writers of these books put so much thought and effort into them, they poured their experiences, emotions, and their very life into them. And I could hoard all of that to myself.

Books are like portals leading to exciting new worlds, it is a great opportunity to be able to explore them. Every time you pick up a book, you are picking up more than just some sheets of inked paper held together with thread or glue.

I'm not saying this because I'm a writer, I'm saying this because a book is months of, if not years of someone's life. You get to experience all of that in however much time you spend reading them. But to experience all of that firsthand would take you much more time than you would take to read a book about it. While nothing can beat practical knowledge and experiences, theoretical knowledge still serves to give you a decent idea about the subject in question, throw your imagination into this mix, and your only limit is you.

23 November 2023

There were chances of me getting late today because I had to wash utensils, feed my dog, and lock up my home after making sure all the switches, taps, and the gas stove were off so that after finishing up with work I don't return to my home half burned down to the ground, or be welcomed by angry and irritated neighbors' because my dog was howling its head off in hunger.

All this because my parents left yesterday night to attend a relative's wedding in the neighboring state. This again reminds me how much work and effort my Mom puts in every day. Household chores aren't the only thing she does, she still works as a teacher, meaning she's always working no matter where she is.

People living on their own, or away from their families will understand this more than those like me who always stayed with their family.

In grade 2 I tried to help my mom with Household chores by washing utensils and sweeping the floor. But my father stopped me, telling me that it was work meant for the women folk and that I shouldn't be doing it. Way to go, Father! I was intimidated and led astray, making me stop trying to help. That was the age of ignorance so it's fine, but I should have helped my mom a few years after that, when I had grown more mature. But no, I was lazy, this doesn't mean I did nothing, I still helped around with a few chores.

Everything you tell and do to a kid while they are growing up impacts how they will turn out in the future. Blaming them for that after they grow up is stupid, you can't expect an Apple tree to sprout from the ground after you planted and religiously watered a Guava seed.

Some of the biases we develop are because of the atmosphere we grow up in. You always have the option to question them as you grow up, see things from your perspective, and form new beliefs, beliefs that are your own.

That bit about only the womenfolk doing the housework is regressive. It is a cultural and social influence affecting people to this day. Back in those days men could only go out and work peacefully because women did all the housework. Even then the women did a lot of work excluding the household chores. Doing household chores and raising kids is no simple task. Switch roles and find out if you ever feel doubtful about that.

The era in which only Men were the sole breadwinners is long gone. Times have changed now. Both husband and wife go out and work to sustain their family. In situations like these, if the husband still expects the wife to do all the house chores, there's no measuring that level of idiocy. The entire concept of a family is wasted on the likes of people like that. Even if you can't do half the work in your home, giving a helping hand whenever possible goes a long way in both strengthening relationships and keeping the atmosphere at your home serene.

Times change, situations change, and as the world is constantly evolving and progressing, our thinking should adapt to accommodate these changes. Holding on to a past practice unquestioningly is like perching atop a lightning rod during severe thunderstorms.

I'm only able to write peacefully because my Mom is doing the chores around the home. This whole thing about household chores is not me trying to coerce you into doing them, I simply wanted you to know that for every comfort we indulge in, there is a cost to be paid, often by someone else.

It is very easy to show someone in a bad light, especially when you are the one with all the lights. From what you read so far, you could easily say my father was that one constant pain point for me. Anything you read ahead in this book won't change that narrative either, it will in fact add more to solidify that.

But whatever you are reading is from my perspective, so you don't see my father's. He wanted me to have a good life, and everything that he did was to ensure that. Although most of that might have backfired, he thought he was right, he still thinks he's right and refuses to view it from any other angle.

If you ever feel your parents are pulling you down or restricting you, talk to them about it, they are not as unreasonable as my father is, that much I can guarantee. If you never tell them, they will never know, and they will keep doing whatever they have been doing.

No parent would want to hurt their children (unless their wiring upstairs is faulty), they are simply overbearing, and try to get you that good life which they didn't have. They do to you whatever they feel does you good. Understand their perspective, and try to get them to understand yours. There's no point in squabbling with them, it only ruins your and their mental peace.

Last week I managed to write a bit more because I started writing right from the time I got to the bus stop. But now I part with my phone till it's time for me to get down at a particular stop to switch buses. There's a kid who befriended me sometime during June this year. He's in grade 5 and commutes on the same bus that I take. I give him my phone so that he can play games on it, while I read whatever novel I have in my bag. He didn't go to school last week, that was how I was able to sneak in a few extra words. Now that he's back, I start writing after I switch buses.

You never know when and how you make new friends. At this bus stop, other than this kid and his friend (who is kind of my friend too now), there's an old man who talks to me. But unlike this kid, he rarely travels, so I don't meet him often.

This bus stop introduced me to these kids who are less than half my age and an old man who is more than double my age. They make for intriguing travel companions, one pair of eyes looks out of the window in innocent curiosity, while the other looks out in tired reminiscence. They couldn't be any more different from each other, yet they very much resemble one another. Both have an aura of helpless restlessness, both spite and love openly, to them this world is a mystery that they lack the resources to change.

I want to say more about them, but the infinite world of words granted me letters for just this one sentence- The duality of life sits by the window seat.

Why I let that kid play games on my phone is more than something as simple as kind-heartedness. I and games go back a long way, we have as much history as I have with books. If books took me to new and intriguing worlds, games allowed me to explore the darkest depths of our actual world.

During grade 3 I used to watch my cousin play games on my uncle's PC. To be more specific it was a game called Destruction Derby, I'm surprised that I still remember its name when I only ever played it once.

In grade 5, my cousin got his own PC, that was the moment when I got both into computers and games. Every vacation I spent at my grandmother's home, I was either reading or playing games.

During the holidays I used to wake up at 4 AM every day to play games on my cousin's PC.

Every time I use the word "cousin" in this book, I'm referring to your dad, there's no other cousin with whom I associated or is worth mentioning. And so, I used to play till it was time for breakfast, after finishing the meal I'd go back to playing till it was time for lunch, then I'd do the same till dinner time, Any breaks in between were compensated by reading books, thus ended my day.

Games, in general, teach you a lot of things, they instill in you a new way of problem-solving and management. Some offline games taught me history effortlessly, while the online games I played were a completely different story.

Every game had a different kind of player base- some toxic, some helpful, some tricking the new players into getting banned, while some tried to scam you out of our gaming account. I had something to learn from everyone. They talked about their life, their country, and their culture. Everything was every bit as fascinating as a fresh page of a fantasy book.

I learned of hardships and misfortunes people have been through which no one should have to go through again. I was in awe of how rich people could be and how vain their lifestyles were. There were people throwing tens of thousands of dollars on a money-grabbing excuse of a game. Then there were kind folks, absolute strangers who were willing to buy me games because I couldn't afford to, it didn't sit right with me to accept charity, so I refused, thanking them for their kind thoughts.

So many kids my age and younger had things and privileges that I could only dream of, if I had just 5% of what they had, it would have made me unimaginably happy back then. Yet these kids always whined about how depressed they were while being cooped up in their expensive gaming rooms.

If we think of the things we don't have, we'll have so much more than any list could fit, but if we take one good look at what we have, we will have more than plenty.

There's just no end to greed.

There will always be someone more fortunate than you, and at the same time, there will be someone less fortunate than you too. When you can be jealous by looking at the former, you can also heave a sigh of relief for being in a better state than the latter.

If you need someone to be miserable for you to feel better, or if you feel miserable by seeing someone who's better, you aren't even living your life. You are letting your life be whatever others want it to be. Like a runaway kite on a windy evening.

24 Nov 2023

I'm thinking, sifting through my memories to find something to tell you about.

I pulled just the right thing. I'll tell you how I started writing. But before that, I'll tell you about the ambitions I had in the past.

Starting from grade 5 our teachers used to ask us about what we wanted to be when we grew up. Teacher, Doctor, Nurse, Police, Army officer, Pilot, and a few other well-respected professions were the answers often repeated by most kids.

But there were two that stood out, one kid wanted to be a software engineer, I don't remember who said it, their mother was probably an Oracle because that kid would now definitely be a software engineer.

The other answer was "The Prime Minister," I remember the kid who said this, he's still my friend. He isn't a Prime Minister yet, but someday he may become one, but for now, he hasn't come of age yet. He isn't even qualified to become a politician yet. He is not old or senile enough. He does not have any police cases filed against him, forget having enough wealth for the next 5 generations, he does not even have enough wealth to last him for the next 5 years.

Just uttering the word "Politics" sours my palate, they are not all despicable people, but most of them are.

Anyway, now that I have told you what other kids used to say, I'll tell you what I said. I used to say I wanted to be a scientist. I wanted to invent new gadgets, build feature-packed vehicles, and design deadly weapons, hence that ambition. During grade 1 I used to tell my parents I wanted to be a truck driver when I grew up, after some time it was a Road Roller, whatever was the biggest vehicle I laid my eyes on, I wanted to become a driver of that. Fortunately, I strayed away from this path before I got to trains and airplanes.

Later on, dismantling toys and broken gadgets became a hobby. I was careful not to experiment with the toys I had, I fed this hobby of mine with only my sister's unsuspecting toys.

After I read Sherlock Holmes, I wanted to be a detective. Then I wanted to join DRDO and develop weapons for our country. But from school to PUC, my ambition remained unchanged, I said Scientist whenever anyone asked me.

Only during PUC did I learn that you don't become something just because you want to, you have to work towards what you want to be. I saw no clear path to becoming a scientist, the mathematical prowess required was beyond me. So I sealed it up in a bottle of bitterness, weighted it with the rock of rationality, and flung it into the sea that was society, to drown with other discarded dreams.

My reading habit often enticed me to write, I finally gave in to it in grade 5. I picked up a short notebook and set out to write the best adventure novel in existence, but this grand ambition was too big for that small book, it died down within four pages.

Here too my dad interfered, he asked me what I was doing, and I told him I was writing a novel. He said it was useless, and I would waste my life if I continued, so I should focus on my studies instead of that. This demotivation and my inherent laziness worked together to keep me from venturing into that path for some time.

But an opportunity came knocking very soon. In grade 6 we were asked to subscribe to the student edition of the Times of India newspaper in our school. That newspaper had a few pages that exclusively featured student pieces. We just had to mail them our work. The next time I went to my grandmother's home I mailed them a poem about friendship.

In the next week, my classmates showed me my poem featured in the newspaper. I was happy, my teachers were too, my mother was overjoyed, and my dad... I didn't care. I didn't want anyone's acknowledgment, just getting it published was the end goal.

Next year it was a short article, the Times of India editorial wanted us to write about our opinion about a controversial publicity stunt a celebrity had pulled. I submitted a short piece condemning what they did. It got published, and my school headmaster was pleased, I got similar reactions to the first time. My dad was angry, he said I shouldn't have written about it because they were powerful people and they could come after me for criticizing them.

I got another poem published in the newspaper the next year, and that was it. Apart from this, I tried writing another book in grade 10, this time it was about the rich heritage of India, I wrote one page, and the rest is missing history.

My English teacher in grade 6 or 7 asked me if she would see my name on the cover of a book sometime in the future. I smiled it off, I didn't have an answer then, and I don't have an answer now. But I'll definitely send her the answer when I have it. If you are reading this Vibha ma'am, you have your answer. (Please forgive me for any grammatical sins I may have committed, I couldn't afford an editor).

Throughout all these writing encounters in school, I never said I wanted to be a writer, but I wanted to write and get my book published.

In all my entire school life there was not a single teacher who had punished me. Unless the entire class was getting caned for making too much noise, there was not a single instance of me being thrown out of the class or getting caned. But that time arrived soon, in grade 7, for the first time, I was thrown out of the class by my art teacher, and it was for no reason at all. There were me and two other classmates standing outside the class in disbelief. They couldn't believe what had happened to me either, one of them tried talking to the teacher about this and got yelled at.

I was angry, being punished was one thing, but being punished when there was no fault of mine made my anger multiply manifold. That whole day I was seething with rage in deadly silence. I wanted revenge for this injustice and humiliation. The first thing I did after going home that day was pull out a small notebook hidden deep within my shelf. I cleanly wrote down her name in that book.

Before you jump to any conclusions, let me clarify that I didn't do any voodoo black magic rituals or practice any arts of witchcraft, and neither do I now. That book was my Vendetta Note. I wrote down the names of my targets here against whom I wanted to exact my revenge.

It would have made for a much more interesting read if I had filled out multiple pages with names in my Vendetta note and set out to teach them a lesson that they will carry to their next life.

25 Nov 2023

Major Spoiler Alert: I only ever wrote down three names in that book, and I didn't exact revenge against any of them.

The Vendetta note came into existence sometime in grade 5. I don't remember what inspired me to start it, it could have been a book that I read.

Whatever its origin story, the first name I wrote on it was of a relative, he was my age. Sometime during Kindergarten when he visited my grandparents' home with his parents, he stole my car. It was a matchbox car, a Jeep, I loved playing with it. But he had to steal just that... He got married just two days ago, but I didn't go attend it.

The second name I wrote in my Vendetta note was my father's and for obvious reasons.

The third is that teacher's.

Depending on how you view it, Procrastination and Revenge make for a very bad duo. Given enough time, Procrastination smothers down the burning flames of Revenge.

That teacher quit teaching a couple of years later after she got some heart issues. I didn't have to do anything, her karma came for her. As for the other two targets, I'm sure they have suffered as well. That thieving relative of mine has Hemophilia, there's no point in plotting revenge against someone the likes of him. And my dad, he'll get his due, I don't have to do a thing. He already regrets forcing me to study Engineering.

I'm not a Sadist, but I did find a little pleasure in their pain, it was because they deserved every bit of it, and I didn't have to waste my energy trying to get back at them.

Revenge is a sweet dish, but too much of it will make you diabetic. I know this was in particularly bad taste, but who's stopping me?

I would exact revenge if I could do it instantly, or without having to spend too much of my time or energy on it. I consider it an option only because of how cathartic and satisfying it is. Many great people in the past and present advocate against it because of how self-destructive it is, they say it is not worth it.

I would say they are barely correct because, A- I'm not a great person like them, and B- The satisfaction of teaching people a lesson when they think they are untouchable is not something that is easily matched by anything else. If you don't show them the consequences of their way, they will go on doing it. We can't always wait for karma to sweep the dirt off the floor, sometimes you have to take that broom into your own hands, sometimes you have to become Karma incarnate itself.

If you feel I'm taking this revenge talk too personally, think again, revenge is and will always be personal. I'm not telling you I want to hurt random strangers or innocent people. I'm only talking about retaliation, responding in kind. Revenge is a reactionary action, it is not something that you initiate, it is something you respond with.

So why is Vengeance bad? It isn't, it's not good either. Vengeance is simple, it has a price tag, and you can either afford it or you cannot.

If you have to spend a lot of time and energy to get back at someone, that revenge is meaningless, you will be hurting yourself more than the person you set out to hurt, and that's plain idiotic.

It's about balancing things out, you'll learn it soon enough if you haven't already.

There's one more thing, it's about what comes after you have had your revenge. I won't talk of the supposed regrets or misgivings in the aftermath. Because if you did feel any of those, that revenge would be meaningless, you don't deserve to exact revenge, just whine about the sufferings you are undergoing and seek sympathy from the world.

Now let's talk about what actually comes after Revenge. After you went ahead and retaliated, do you think your target would pass it off saying, "Oh! He's having his revenge, let him teach me a lesson for I have wronged him"? Maybe in some weird dream. In reality, they will come after you again, and try to put you in your rightful place.

I don't want any hassle, so if I did take revenge, I would do so only after making sure my target wouldn't get back at me. And in the off chance they did, I would have a backup plan to deal with them.

This is the cost I talked about, if you can't afford it, then don't even think about it.

Then there are people against whom revenge is wasted. They are people who are accelerating on a path to their self-annihilation. You don't have to do anything, just wait and watch them set explosives under their own seat.

Revenge is the firstborn child of anger and humiliation. During the course of my entire school life, the former was a distant relative, and the latter a stranger knocking on my door.

I was rarely angry during that period, I would laugh it off. There was plenty of anger going around in my house already, between the angry outbursts of my father and the temper tantrums of my sister, I didn't want to add further steam to the already screaming teapot.

My Anger from then was mostly of just one kind- The Righteous kind. If you are wondering how Anger can be right or wrong, this might hopefully clear it up. Anger is probably the most honest of all emotions. Because of that exact reason, I'm able to classify it into certain types. I'll tell you about them tomorrow.

27 Nov 2023

Since we were previously discussing Revenge it is only right to start with Vengeful Anger. As the name suggests, this is something closely linked to revenge. This is the anger that pushes you to take revenge, numbing you to logic in the process. Unless it is channeled or controlled, the price of your revenge will go up drastically.

28 Nov 2023

If you want revenge, you will have better chances without the Vengeful anger acting as your accomplice.

Helpless Anger- the anger born out of being unable to affect the situation. The most common, the most stupidest, and the most easily quellable anger. There might have been, and there will be hundreds of scenarios where the situation is unfavorable to you, and you mostly can't do a thing to change it (without incurring significant costs). At times like these, anger instinctively arises, clouding all senses of rationality, as storm clouds do to the sun. The higher your sense of rationality, the lower the chance of you getting controlled by your anger.

You wake up late, and now you are angry at your mom because she told you to eat your breakfast but you don't have the time for that, you are cursing the taxi driver because he's taking his sweet time getting there.

A person in a position of power insults you, but you can't do a thing, the rest of your day is ruined, and you are angry, irritable, and grumbling the whole day.

You miss your bus, it starts raining, you are soaked to the skin, your mom calls you asking where you are, and you start shouting at her.

You are booking tickets at the last moment, the app is buggy, and at the last moment, there's a payment error. You grind your teeth in anger, you are inches away from destroying that display.

The team you were supporting/you were playing for lost, now you start abusing your team players, the opposite team, the umpire, and whoever else you can blame.

In all these situations, there is very little you can do. Anger is the last thing that will help you here, why then dance to its hypnotic beats of destruction? Once you realize the "Why?" It will be completely powerless against you. If you can't change it, why waste your energy on it?

Righteous Anger- this is a derivative of helpless anger, but it is not thoughtless, destructive, irresponsible, or short-lived like helpless anger. It is thoughtful, constructive, responsible, and stays with you for a long time, so long that it starts to live with you. It is borne of the helpless aspiration to do good. This anger is directed at everyone in society for turning a blind eye to the unjust and immoral acts taking place around them. It is directed at yourself for being helpless, for not being able to do more to bring about a change and set things right. More than for you, it is for the sake of others that you are angered. Channeling this will take you a long way, and fill you with near-limitless energy because you have cast away self, the last limiter of a human being.

We can make further classifications, but it will be a drag. If you are interested in more, look it up online, there is sure to be plenty of material with supporting research and even whole books on this topic.

You can more or less segregate all types of anger in the above three, I will surely have missed something major but I don't remember it and I don't want to check online. So that is that. Let's go to the next form of Anger- Rage.

Rage is rage, you lose control and let your anger take over, end of the story. Don't be so weak as to let it take over. You won't be fighting in a life-or-death moment where your rage will help you kill multiple enemies like in movies, you will get dropped in seconds. Stay calm and live to fight another day.

It is never a good idea to let any one of your feelings take complete control, the result will always be horrifying. You have lost the moment you feel rage.

Anger can be used like adrenaline to surge forward and get things done, but that is only if you can control it, if it's the other way around, the repercussions will be more than simple fatigue.

Anger isn't your enemy, it's a deadly weapon. You will have to learn to use it on the right target and in the right situations, or you will end up hurting yourself.

29 Nov 2023

What or who are you angry at and why? Ask yourself this question when you get angry, most of the time, the answer is unflatteringly you. Don't lie, don't shift the blame. Why take it out on someone else? If it truly is because of someone else, why would you allow them to control your emotions, why let them control you?

I told you that during my school time, the only anger I felt was Righteous anger. In grade 5 I finally learned the full meaning of the word "Corruption," the name of my Archenemy. Back then, my sense of justice was fierce and strong, I wanted to eradicate corruption, and every other evil in the society.

Whenever any teacher asked us to write an essay on what we wanted to be when we grew up, I'd write about eliminating corruption and making this world a better place.

I was angry whenever I saw people throw garbage on the road and dirtied public places. I was angry when I saw news of politicians and other government employees being arrested for bribery. I was angry when I read articles about brutal rapes and killings in the newspaper. I was angry when I saw disabled, young, and old people begging on the streets. I was angry when political parties played their appeasement games ignoring the important issues at hand. I was angry when they dug up roads just weeks after their construction. I was angry at all the public money being wasted to provide luxury to worthless vermin. I was angry when schools and other public institutions still asked for caste and religion in application forms. I was angry at the undeserving people getting opportunities. I was angry at all the country's talent flying away abroad, and seeing how their acts were justified made me angrier. I was angry at the society as a whole for not doing anything. I was angry at myself for not being able to do anything.

Now I'm just angry for not doing anything.

This transition may or may not surprise you depending on how long you have lived. It is surprising how a little life can alter everything.

You would be mistaken if you thought all this anger would make you rage like an exploding volcano. No, it instead brought forth a strange sense of calmness. It heightens your focus and clears your mind of every single distracting thought. It is that figurative calm before the storm, and if you can keep the storm at bay, everything comes to a standstill, it's an ocean of deathly calm. You have drifted into the flow state before you even realize it. You can exploit this anger to get things done, this is your mind's little cheat code.

Maybe I didn't lose my temper and get angry at silly things during my school days because I was mostly possessed by Righteous anger. So there was no space or scope for any other type of anger, or maybe not.

Speaking of anger anymore might make you angry, so I'll drop it for now.

I'll tell you something else instead, a tidbit about your parents. When I was enjoying my school vacations, your dad had to attend college, because the more you grow up, the fewer your holidays become. On one such holiday, a couple of his friends had come over. Your mom was one of them. She was teaching me to call her "Vadina," which means sister-in-law in Telugu. I don't know if they remember this now, but I do.

My mind is a blank, I'm trying to think of what to write next. I can't remember anything else interesting from my school life.

It has been 45 minutes since I got to the bus stop, the me from a month ago would be irritated because of the amount of time being wasted. But the me right now doesn't care, I'm at least getting time to write. When you can't change the situation, you can change the way you react to it instead. It will make a whole lot of difference.

I stuck to my usual study methods and scored 9.2 out of 10 CGPA in grade 10. That was 2nd rank in my class. Grade 10 results were considered very important because your admission to PUC or Diploma college depended on them.

Here's the deal, when we were in grades 1-5, grade 6 was considered very important, when we got to grade 7, grade 8 was supposed to be very important so we were made to study more seriously. Then we got to grade 8, they said your entire life depended on grade 10. After we got into PUC they told us everything so far was inconsequential, and the 2nd year of PU would dictate the course of your life. After that, we got into engineering, and they said our previous educational ranks and merits were for naught, the real-life changers were supposed to be these 4 years of engineering. After finishing 4 years of hardcore engineering, they said we had zero skills to be recruited, so we had to skill up by joining additional courses by paying hefty amounts to third-party institutions that promised handsome placement offers once we finished their training program.

I left this rat race after I finished my engineering, but I'll continue with the rest of that cycle which I have second-hand experience of. With barely a month to a maximum of three months of those extra courses, almost all of my engineering batchmates got jobs in the corporate world.

This was not to showcase the awesome abilities of those training institutes, they only taught basic coding skills, which some of my friends gained just by watching videos on YouTube. It is about that entire rat race we ran through. Now whenever I view it as a whole, I only see hamsters running on a wheel. This is absolutely pitiful and mind-numbing. The only ones benefiting from all of this are the huge amounts of educational institutions, training and coaching centers, and stationery manufacturers. And of course, the employers getting cheap labor at the end of this cycle.

Whoever came up with all of this, my humble salutations to you-oh Genius of modern Torture, Sadist Supreme, Ruiner of Education, Trampler of Talents, Tester of Patience, Manufacturer of Mindless Minions, The Unholy Master of the Unmeritorious, and the countless holder of titles that would make even Satan commit seppuku out of shame, I stand firm and hold my head high to you in disrespect.

9.2 CGPA is a decent score, almost all colleges in the city where I lived should ideally have welcomed me to join them as a student. Earlier I had mentioned that all the educational institutions were affiliated with different boards, I studied in a CBSE-affiliated school, and then there were State board affiliated schools and ICSE board schools. The state board students got their results almost a month before us. This meant they could go to colleges and gain admissions before we could, and they did. Colleges accept or pretend to accept only a limited number of student admissions, once they are all sold out, only a significant amount of money can open the doors for you. We didn't have a significant amount of money, so I was admitted to a half-decent college whose principal was very happy to have me.

I barely attended it for a week, I got admission into one of the top colleges, so I bid this college goodbye and switched to the new college.

The one week I had attended that half-decent college gave me mixed feelings about PUC education. There was an overly rude teacher, who was straight out verbally abusing students on the first day. He told us not to feel good about scoring good grades in grade 10, it was no achievement, and all of that was useless. That semi-bald bastard, excuse my language, if only he had said that to us during school.

Anyway, the new college didn't give me much to remember. It boasted of alumni who are currently celebrities, this didn't mean anything to me. But it gave me an opportunity to start anew, I took not wanting to gain attention to a whole new level. Our class had almost a hundred students, so it helped me big time. I sat on the first or second bench and had over 95% attendance, yet I barely existed. Most people in my class didn't even know I was from their own class.

I'll stop here for the day. Talk to you tomorrow.

30 Nov 2023

In PUC, we had five teachers for mathematics, four for chemistry, three for physics, two for electronics, three for English (two in the 2nd year), and two for Hindi (one in the 2nd year). We had classes six days a week, Saturday was a half day i.e. around 5 hours, and the rest of the weekdays were around 8 hours.

We had math classes 5 days a week, a different teacher came in to teach us each day, and each of them taught us a different topic picked from the prescribed syllabus. It was the same with every other subject. Such an ingenious way of covering the syllabus.

That was when I lost all remaining interest in education. I thought I'd be taught something interesting, but no it was just more memorization mania. Just gobble up all the things from your textbooks and vomit them on your answer papers in the tests. You didn't have to do anything else. The only thing these tests tested was your patience.

My social teacher in school gave me a good lesson, she showed me how brutal reality was. She was our sole teacher for the social science subjects from grade 7 to 9. She used to cut my marks for no reason. She wanted the text to be written the exact same way it appeared in our textbooks. I never did that for any subject, I understood the textbook and answered the questions. I didn't copy-paste the answers we were given in class. I couldn't memorize well, so this was my only way.

It worked throughout my school life and for almost all subjects too. Mathematics was the only issue because I didn't quite understand all the algebra and trigonometry. After all, they needed formulae, and the formulae you had to memorize. It was the same with parts of chemistry that required you to memorize molecular weights, atomic numbers, and other constants.

How are the atomic weights of noble gases helping me right now? I don't know, maybe the education minister and the people who set the syllabus have some answers. I a lowly human can't hold a torch to their erudite genius. Only high-IQ intellectuals whose brains function in similar wavelengths might be able to understand the logic behind this grand scheme.

Luckily for me, we got a new social teacher in grade 10, and my grades in the social science subjects improved significantly, I was finally scoring marks worth my answers.

In PUC I barely got passing grades, the only subject where my score was anywhere near the 90s was English. The rest of the marks were cut because I didn't fill my answer paper with nonsense. For 5 marks you were supposed to write 10+ pages, in what world does that make sense? Even the author whose work that question is based on would be surprised by the tens of pages worth of answers the students were writing. The author would go- "I didn't myself know that this measly line held this deep of a meaning."

My Hindi scores were not too bad either, I used to get around 70%. Now, before I continue I'll tell you about the different streams you could pick in PUC. You have Science, Arts, and Commerce. If you choose science, you get three more choices- PCME, PCMC, and PCMB. P is Physics, C is Chemistry, and M is Mathematics, these are common whatever you pick. Now come the core subjects- E is Electronics, C is Computer Science, and B is Biology.

Again, whatever you pick, you get two languages with it. I don't know of the arts and commerce streams, they were ignored in general, and parents usually wanted their kids to pursue science so that they could become doctors or engineers.

In the first year, I barely escaped failing. I cleared it somehow, my father was not very pleased with the results. He blamed my Novel reading and PC gaming activities for it. He never did like me reading novels in the first place. During school times I had to hide away from him to read. Whatever book I was currently reading would be hidden under my pillow, when we all went to sleep (we slept early), I would read the book in the night light till I felt sleepy.

I read a good number of books during the first year of PUC, but after that, I couldn't get away with hiding and reading books anymore. My reading habit slowly fell into ruin. I don't remember reading any non-academic books while in my second year of PUC.

At the end of the first year holidays, a ghost from my past came to visit. I tried to freelance, and some random person hired me to write for their website, I wrote an article about pets, and he liked it and consequentially published it on his site. When it came to payment, he said he couldn't pay me because I wasn't 18 yet, The End. The ghost went back to the graveyard.

There was a fairly large library in our college, but even with its thousands of books, it looked quite bare to me. In my previous exploration, I discovered that it was filled with only academic text. The only things there that could remotely be identified as books were magazines. I read tech magazines and newspapers there whenever I had spare time.

That was me disrespecting books, I apologize, books are books, there are no good or bad books. Those in that library, I just didn't like, they weren't my type, but they would definitely help a lot of other people. I won't call them trash, but then again, one man's trash is another's treasure.

Enough trash talk. I'm doubting this whole book now. Will it even help you if you decide to read it someday in the far future? All this talk, I'm not sure if it is making any sense, I could be rambling and ranting for all I know. Whatever the answer, I have come too far, and I have never come this far before. It would be a waste to turn back now, I'll see it to the end, for once.

I had second thoughts about getting this published too, it would barely sell ten copies, and those ten would be bought by the people I know. So I thought I would just get one book printed and gift it to you, then again comes the question of preservation. The whole reason behind getting it published was to make it available to you whenever and wherever you are. I'll have to think about it again after I finish writing and editing this book.

You are what is keeping me writing, If you are reading this, Thank You.

In my 2nd year of PUC, I broke my arm, this was in September. This incident involved a bus depot, a bus, me walking on a narrow sidewalk, a wall, and bad timing. Half my body would have been crushed if I hadn't used my hand, thanks to that I fractured my radius, and dislocated my thumb and wrist. It was a small price to pay. I knew it the moment I heard a crack, it hurt, but it wasn't intolerable. I had three choices now.

1 Dec 2023

Choice 1: I could break down in pain and hope for some random passerby to take me to a hospital.

Choice 2: My grandmother's home was nearby (1.3 kilometers away). I could either call my aunt or go there myself with the help of an Autorickshaw.

Choice 3: I could wait for the next bus home.

Choice 1 wasn't even a choice for me, it was against my character traits, so I didn't even consider it. Choice 2 was a feasible option, the logical thing to do. But my grandparents and aunt would panic, especially my aunt, I would be putting her in more pain than I was in. Calling them would worry them to no end. Going there on my own with an injury like this would shock them. So I did the thing I do best- I went home.

I waited some time for the bus, it could have been 5 minutes, or it could have been 20, I couldn't remember. Pain alters your perception of time, it drives you into its dimension of desperation, raining down suffering on the weak-willed.

When the bus finally arrived, there were a lot of people competing for seats, I somehow pushed in through the crowd and got myself a seat. The slightest movement of my right arm hurt. I tried to keep it steady, but the pothole-filled road with random speed breakers wasn't helping at all. I dozed off for a bit, and when I awoke I realized I had missed my stop. I got down at the next stop and boarded a bus back to the place where I had to go, luckily I hadn't gone too far. I got down at my usual stop this time, I had to walk around a kilometer and a half to get to my home from there. I found an autorickshaw and paid for a ride home instead. As much as I liked to walk, now wasn't the time for it.

I got home, my father had hired a carpenter and they were constructing a bed in the yard. This was the very reason I had to go home that day, If not I would be at my grandmother's home. That day was a Saturday, September 3 2016 to be precise. It was two days before Ganesh Chaturthi, every consequent year before this I went to my grandmother's home, either on the festival day or a day before it, depending on when we got holidays. This was to help with decoration and celebrate the festival there. It was the same that year too, I was supposed to go to my aunt's place on that Saturday, the festival was on Monday. But my father had specifically instructed me to not go there and come home instead. If not for having to go home, I wouldn't even have gone to that bus depot. I didn't blame him though, it was an unexpected event.

Acting all normal I passed by my father and went inside. After pulling a few acrobatic maneuvers I managed to change my clothes. Then I sat down on the sofa and told my mom- “My arm is broken.” She asked how. I cooked up a story about how while boarding the bus my arm hit one of the poles inside the bus, and because of the crowd pushing me around strongly, my bone fractured due to the impact. It was a silly way to get your arm broken. I didn’t then tell her the truth because of how complicated it was to explain the actual incident, and also because of the danger involved. She called my father inside, I repeated the same lie. He scolded me for being careless and weak.

My relatives were pitying me for being unlucky to get injured like that. After a couple of weeks, I told my mom the truth, she agreed when I said I got lucky that time.

I stayed home without having to go to college for almost 3 months. There was a mid-term exam in November or December, I can’t exactly remember when. The college principal and other faculty said it was fine if I didn’t take the exam because it did not amount to anything. It wouldn’t affect my final grade either. But my father insisted on me writing it, my right hand was in no state to write, so my college principal told us we could get someone to write for me while I dictated to them. My cousin was that person.

We wasted a week by going to college every day, scribbling a few sentences, and coming back home. I failed multiple subjects, and I think I scored 4 or 5 marks out of 70 in mathematics. The lowest score I had ever gotten in anything, and this was the first time I had failed an exam. This was an expected outcome, there were no surprises, I already knew I would fail while on the way to write the exam. Not only my time but my cousin’s was wasted too.

Here’s another college anecdote, we were taught integration before we even learned differentiation, unfortunately, the limit of stupidity tends to be infinite. All of this because of that five teachers for maths thing. I’m trying so hard not to antagonize the education system, but it keeps pushing me, I'm still trying to keep criticism to the minimum.

Because of my poor performance in the previous year, my father forcefully got me enrolled in a coaching center at the beginning of the 2nd year of PUC. My college fee was 18k a year, while the coaching center charged around 60k. They took classes for only two hours a day. They had good teachers, but they didn't teach anything from the basics, they assumed we already had enough info from our college classes, which I didn't have. In college, they assumed we all went to coaching centers when they taught us, so I ended up understanding neither. I told my father that I didn't want to join a coaching class, and he didn't listen. A good amount of money and time went down the drain.

2 Dec 2023

In the 2nd year of PUC, I started wearing spectacles. I needed them then, I needed them since grade 6 in school, but I was afraid my father would scold me for that. In school I managed without them by sitting on the first bench in the class and squinting my eyes, if I still couldn't see something clearly, I would copy down the notes from the students sitting beside me.

This cost me a contest too. From grade 6 to 10 I participated in a lot of quiz contests, I cleared multiple rounds, but I either lost in the final round or the one before that. The first round for these contests was usually the school round, you were given a question and answer sheet. But for this particular contest, the management messed up and didn't print the question papers. So they instead got a projector and gathered all the students from grades 4 to 10 in our school seminar hall. I was sitting some 6 or 7 meters away from the screen where the questions were being displayed. No amount of squinting would allow me to see that far when in our classroom I had a hard time seeing the things on the blackboard just 2 meters away.

In my first year of PUC, I had a tough time reading the route numbers on buses when they were approaching the bus stop, and when inside the classroom it was the same story, I would copy down notes from those sitting beside me. In the holidays after the end of 1st year of PUC, I decided I had fooled around enough and got spectacles. The moment I put on those glasses everything was so clear. This clear vision seemed like a privilege. I should have done this years ago. If I had, my eyesight wouldn't have further deteriorated.

This is definitely a lesson for you. If you have any health issues, tell your parents ASAP, don't delay it. The more you delay treating them, the worse they will get, so don't ignore it. If for some reason you feel like you can't tell your parents, then tell me if I'm still around. I'll do what I can. This is not just about your health, you can tell me of whatever problems you have.

I cleared my 2nd year PUC with 59%, I had scored just enough marks to obtain a passing grade in maths, the rest were in the 60s, and English in the 70s. I didn't care, but you know who did, and he was extremely displeased and angry.

Right after I obtained the results, the verbal abuses started. I was at my grandparents' home at that time, and my aunt was there along with my dad when I was checking the results. If not for her I would have received a few beatings too. There was a brief break in the river of abuses, he had paused to ask my aunt to enquire from me what I planned to do next. I said, I would like to do a degree in literature, biotechnology, or some other field, and my aunt backed me up too. His anger flared, he said he didn't get me to pursue science in PUC to get worthless degrees like these, if you studied science you had to do engineering next. End of the discussion, to cement this point he threw a chair at me, and I deflected it away by reflex. There were no more arguments.

This obsession with Engineering was because of social pressure, everyone was getting their children to study Engineering because they believed software engineers were swimming in money. Even now things haven't changed much. Because of all this peer pressure and herd mentality, the Indian job market is oversaturated with underqualified Engineers.

I remembered something from my school time. In grade 7 my parents got me to take an entrance exam for a school. If I passed that exam I would get free education from grade 8 till 2nd PUC. It was a great opportunity, but clearing the exam would mean I would have to live in that school's hostel. The only time I would be coming home was during long vacations. I was touchy about my freedom then, so that hostel idea did not appeal to me in the slightest. The day of the entrance test soon came, and I knew almost all the answers to the questions in the question paper. I took my time to carefully answer all the questions incorrectly because I didn't want to clear that test even by accident. When the results were declared, my mom knew what I had done, she knew I didn't want to go live in a hostel. My father wasn't very impressed, but he didn't pursue the matter any further. My opinion on that matter is the same even now, I don't like them hostels. Forget nice, I have never once heard anyone saying their hostel food was decent.

5 Dec 2023

I have always been a picky eater, I like my food a certain way. If I were to give up all luxuries, my preferred food would be somewhere last in the line. I didn't want fancy food, simple food would suffice as long as they were flavourful. Like thin and crisp dosas right off the pan, perfectly cooked rice with the grains not sticking to your fingers. Curries with the right amount of spice and salt. It goes on and on...

I allow very little to affect me, and food is one of those. There's a saying- "You are what you eat," it is true both physically and mentally. Whatever we eat affects us, the most noticeable changes are the immediate emotional change, and that slight bulge in your stomach. There are plenty of other physical changes based on what and how much you eat. Then some studies say what you eat affects how your body ages. It is an undisputed fact that with proper food and water, you can live a healthy and long life.

If these are some short-term changes caused by food, the long-term impact is simply stunning. Evolution. Based on what diet we stick to, our body changes over time to adapt to that. Our teeth, digestive system, and everything else will change to adapt. If we all ate only meat, our distant descendants' bodies would develop to suit that diet. While evolution takes its own sweet time, your mind can do it instantly. It is almost scary how fast we can adapt to certain things.

Just think about the potential you hold when you have access to an ability like that. Don't tell yourself for even a second you can't do it, you can, and everyone else can too, you only have to will it, and it shall happen.

Food is the sacred nectar that bestows upon us immortality, at the same time, it is a sickly poison that strips us slowly of life. We are fated to turn into nourishment for the very things that nourish us. We are what we eat.

I keep coming back to the same point, now, throughout this book, and outside of it too. It is not my fault, It is life's, ...no, this universe's nature to spiral back to its origin to begin anew.

When I was referring to food previously, you might have thought of the plant or animal matter that we consume. What about the food for your mind? Your thoughts? Now run through everything you read with this perspective, need I say anymore?

Earlier I said that food is one of the very few things that I let affect me, let's go back to grade 6 for a while. It was during the lunch break, I was eating my lunch religiously, and my friend was saying something, I told him to speak after he finished eating, but he had to blabber while chewing his food, it was disgusting, I still feel the same way when people do that. Back then I rarely got angry, but this was the tipping point. I twisted his arm, held it to his back, and let him taste my fist of fury. My anger soon dissipated, I apologized, but I told him it was his fault for not heeding my warning. He understood that clearly, furthermore, I wasn't the type to pick fights, so he knew he had really gone and pushed all the wrong buttons. His arm was sore for a few days, but he learned a valuable lesson in return. I hope he hasn't reverted back to his old ways, if he has, then I pray for him to choke on his food. That was the first and last time I hit someone.

If you studied basic biology, you would know better than to talk while eating. Choking on your food and dying is an embarrassing way to go, it will make for a funny obituary though. So, by all means, choke and die, but don't do it near me, it is disgusting.

With all this said, you should get a clearer understanding of why I didn't want to go to a hostel.

6 Dec 2023

My mathematics score in PU should have been reason enough to not let me anywhere near an Engineering college. But alas, if people were that easy to reason with, the world would be a completely different place. Unfortunately many among us choose to walk blindfolded with the garb of emotion, completely blind to the light of logic.

If herd mentality was one contributing factor, the other is disrespect towards other professions and insecurity of your own. My father is an Autorickshaw driver, before that, he was working as a supervisor under an engineer. Since he worked under an engineer, and because of all the enormous amount of unrealistic bullshit about engineers floating about among his social circles, he decided on what would be the best for me- Engineering.

If you don't respect your profession, you can't expect anyone else to respect it either. It is not self-degrading, or shameful to do honest hard work. You should only be ashamed if you did something wrong, like robbing, threatening, or resorting to some other uncivilized means.

You are a driver, so what? Respect your passengers, be humble, but don't be subservient. There's a huge difference between the two. Your passenger could be the prime minister, what does that change? The prime minister will do their job, you do yours. No profession is above or below yours. Every profession is like a cog in a machine, some small, some big, but without doubt, every cog is important, with just one missing, the entire machine could malfunction.

Now about the other professions, my father was degrading his own and countless other professions, because Engineers were supposed to be superior to them in his perspective. But are they really? They might make more money, they might work in air-conditioned rooms, and they might talk all fancy and dress up like it is their birthday every day. But that doesn't mean anything. If you respect a particular profession because of the amount of money it makes, you should idolize politicians, scammers, thieves, and other money grubbers, because what engineers make is less than pocket change to them. If you are respecting a profession, it should be because of the work they do.

There are many people here who look at Garbage collectors, and sewage cleaners, in a demeaning manner. My only question to them is can you do better what they are doing? Forget better, can you even do what they are doing? If you can't, then how are you better than them?

7 Dec 2023

Having more money than someone else doesn't make you better than them, it only makes you wealthier than them, wealthy isn't better. I'm not saying this to stop you from pursuing wealth, wealth has its own significance in this world, but valuing people based on it is not a good idea. People are more than the money they possess.

But then again, do people ever stop pursuing wealth? Once you start making more money, you will start spending more, then you'll want even more money so that you can spend even more, it transforms into a cycle of greed. The pursuit of wealth is not an issue, but the pursuit of limitless wealth is. Strike a balance between what you need and what you want. On one end of the spectrum, you will find yourself transformed into a hermit-like existence, on the other end you are an unrecognizable savage beast.

Thanks to this lure of wealth and respect, I found myself trapped in the cage of Engineering. I didn't take the bait, but I got trapped either way. Thus began my life of Engineering.

An Engineering course is for four years. It has eight semesters, with every year having two semesters. Every semester has four exams, three internal tests, and one external exam. The external aka the final exam of that semester depends on the board or the university the college is affiliated to. The university my college was affiliated with was a big one, it operated only in our state, but it was the biggest, and had a lot of colleges under it. So in our case, the final exam for the semester meant the question paper would be set and sent to our college by that board. Other universities or colleges which were considered private, set their own question papers and conducted the final exam for the semester as they pleased.

In the course of these eight semesters, we had to study, write exams for, and clear 57 subjects. Forget remembering the syllabus of those subjects, I doubt most graduates would even remember the names of those 57 subjects. If someone who is reading this remembers them, then good job! Give yourself a pat on your back.

If exams were one thing, assignments were another. They are the school homework equivalent for college students, pointless, and a waste of time. We were given one assignment per subject before every internal test. We were given marks for submitting assignments, that was the sole driving factor for anyone to write those assignments. These assignments involved us copying and pasting stuff from over the internet and other college notes into our assignment notebooks. My sister helped me write a few assignments because my arm still hurt if I stressed it.

8 Dec 2023

In the first semester, I was doubtful whether I would get a passing grade in mathematics, but luckily I did. But I wasn't so lucky in the second semester, I failed in mathematics. Here's more info before you get confused- We had mathematics in the first four semesters.

The syllabus for the first year of Engineering is common for all branches. There are a good number of branches in Engineering, the most common being- Computer Science, Mechanical, Civil, Electronics, and Electricals.

I picked Electronics again, in the first year we had to study the basics of the C programming language, an electrical subject, a mechanical subject, a civil engineering subject, Physics, Chemistry, Mathematics, Environmental Studies, and of course, a subject from Electronics.

From what I heard, students from all branches had to study all of these unrelated subjects in case anyone wanted to switch their branch after the first year. If this is really the case, they could have just simply removed all those subjects in the first year, that would have been one less year wasted.

The Sadistc part of this whole charade is that we had a Mechanical workshop lab where we were taught welding and basic sheet metal shaping. There was a Civil lab where we were taught basic sketching and CAD. Being electronics students, we learned to weld, and do CAD, but not one laboratory throughout the course of these 4 years, 8 semesters, and 57 subjects taught us anything about soldering electronic circuits. And why we had a chemistry lab, with all those titration tests, and salt analysis, I have not the slightest clue. Don't even get me started on the rest of the subjects, I don't want this book to be about that.

The failure back in PUC was inconsequential, but this wasn't. Failing a subject in engineering meant you had to retake that subject with the upcoming semester's subjects in the next external exam. This is called a "backlog." If you happen to have more than 4 backlogs in an even semester, you will have to repeat that year again, this is called "year back."

I obtained my first backlog in my second semester of engineering. Do you know of Gacha games? Look them up if you don't. Engineering is similar to that of gacha experience. Once you fail a subject, you can either pay the exam fee and write it again in the next exam, or pay the revaluation fee and get it revaluated, if you are lucky you pass, if not, you fail. If you fail, you pay up and write it again. There is another option, but this is almost never used by students who fail a subject. This is instead commonly used by top-ranking students who feel they have gotten fewer marks than they have written for. In that case, they pay the university for a photocopy of their answer sheet.

What's the common factor in all of this? Money. The university found ways to make as much money as possible. My university has around 80,000 students studying under it every year. There are so many other universities and colleges unaffiliated with this, but they all have sophisticated systems just like this to mint money.

I shouldn't be telling you this, but I will anyway. Most of the so-called "big people" in society are not where they are now because of their honesty and hard work. They are there because they exploited and played around with the system. I strongly believe the sentence- "It's not a crime if you don't get caught." If you are capable of outsmarting everyone else, you deserve whatever you have obtained by doing that. Conscience and Morals are yours alone, develop them however you want them to. If you plan to do a crime, don't be stupid enough to get caught, if you are, then don't even think about it.

Karma is your conscience, coincidence, or someone's vengeance masquerading around, reacting to your actions. I already told you about Vengeance. Coincidence- you can't change what you can't change. Conscience- your conscience is yours to command. Now tell me, where or what is Karma?

If Karma can't get you, what else can? The law and your stupidity.

Every student who fails a subject in engineering almost always applies for a revaluation, there's a chance for them to pass this way without having to write it again. Since the odds are not zero it is worth taking the chance (the gacha experience).

While in school and PUC, I studied on the day of the exam at home before leaving for school. In Engineering I took it up a notch, I studied on the day of exams, but only after I reached college. No wonder my grades were almost always on the borderline.

9 Dec 2023

From what we were told by the professors who went out to evaluate papers, the maximum amount of time the evaluators spend evaluating one student's answer sheet is five minutes, that's the maximum allocated time, but most of the time they spend only around two minutes evaluating one student's answer script. This is because they have hundreds of papers to evaluate before the end of the day, and the sooner they finish their quota, the sooner they can leave. So what do the evaluators do? They skim through the answer scripts, matching students' answers to the answers they are given for reference. The icing on the cake is that the professors who go from all the colleges affiliated with the university to evaluate papers are randomly assigned answer scripts. Most of the time they are evaluating subjects that they don't even teach.

This is why filling up answer sheets to increase page count works. For questions with derivations and those that involve finding a mathematical solution, if you manage to memorize the final answer and a couple of steps before that, you get full marks for that. Because that's what the evaluators see most of the time, not the whole process. How were these pathetic exams supposed to test anyone's potential?

I saw someone saying the whole point of education was to instill discipline into the students. It makes perfect sense, what these educational institutes do is manufacture labor that does what they are told, no questions asked.

Have you ever heard of people comparing children to God? They might have a variety of reasons for saying children are closer to God, some even go a step further and call children God. What most have in mind when they compare children to God is the children's innocence, they equate being innocent to being pure, and hence that connection to God.

I believe innocence is ignorance, calling someone innocent is a milder way of calling them ignorant. I don't know God, but I'm willing to bet a couple of my books that God wouldn't be ignorant. I too believe children are closer to God, but it is for an entirely different reason.

If I asked you to tell me any three qualities of children, what would you say? If your answer contains "Curiosity," you should know where I'm going with this one. Everyone is innately curious, but sadly, most people's curiosity wanes with their age.

Children are very curious, they are inquisitive. They want to learn about everything, they devour all available knowledge in their proximity like a gigantic black hole, growing with every new thing they absorb. You could call them an all-accepting singularity. That is why they are closest to God. The path of curiosity always leads to creation.

Don't ever stop asking questions, especially to yourself. Unseen paths and perspectives will open up with every question you ask. It is not always about the answer, the question itself serves a greater purpose. It sets you on a path of discovery and introspection.

The simplest questions are often the hardest to answer, the reason being the various ways in which they can be interpreted. "Who are you?" Tell me this answer if you are reading this.

10 Dec 2023

I saw you for the first time today without data packets having to travel 12,985 kilometers to and fro. You probably won't remember this little encounter, but you were clinging to your grandmother like a gecko to a wall, crying whenever anyone even made eye contact with you.

I was thinking of taking a leave today to spend the day with you, but I can't. I have to get this book finished by your birthday. With you arrived a more defined deadline. I'm not particularly fond of babies, they cry too much and are very fragile, but I'll try not to avoid you.

From the time I started writing while traveling, I have barely written anything while at home. I need to get back that habit soon.

Ever since I left school I haven't turned back to look at it again. So many of my friends reminisce about school days, often mentioning how carefree and exciting those times were, and wishing they could relive them. But never once did I long to be back in school or anytime else in my past, it is not because I didn't like it, it's because where I belong is the present.

11 Dec 2023

During my PUC and Engineering years, I avoided going anywhere near my school, it being just 280 meters from my home didn't help much. I was doing this to avoid running into any of my teachers. They all had great expectations of me, they believed I would achieve something big, and they saw me somewhere high up on a pedestal in the future. What would I say to them if I had met them during these years? Should I have said that I was barely obtaining passing grades? Or That I had joined a subpar Engineering college because of my PUC grades since I couldn't get into any better colleges without having to shell out a fortune? Or That I failed multiple subjects in Engineering? Or that I chose to work a low-paying job and lead a normal life fit for a background character?

It was not Shame that made me avoid my teachers, well... Maybe 4% shame, but the rest of the reason was due to expectations. I didn't want to dash their expectations to the ground, disappoint them, or hurt them. I wouldn't have hesitated to do this to anyone else because I believe it's their fault for having expectations. But with my teachers, it is a completely different story. The life I led in school was such that it would automatically draw in expectations, I didn't do this purposefully, it was something passive that was ingrained into me. Whatever the case, I was responsible for them having high expectations of me. It would be cruel to make them think they were wrong. If I avoided meeting them altogether, they wouldn't know what had become of me, because of their positive bias, they would only assume something good. Their last memory of me would be left intact.

This is almost lying, because I'm delaying or maybe even denying them the truth. I don't like lying, so this is the method I chose. A convenient loophole for me to exploit.

Before I continue, let me sneak in a couple of incidents from my present. In the morning when I was traveling to the office, I saw the same woman whom I had talked about at some point earlier in this book. She had a child with her and was distributing printed sheets, I accepted it this time. I was spot on with my prediction, that piece of paper said that her husband was a laborer who had gotten injured at work, suffering multiple fractures. Because of this, she had to take care of her child and injured husband all on her own, which is why she was requesting monetary aid from strangers in this way.

Not a single person was reaching for their wallet to give her money. I thought I would give her money and try a social experiment at the same time. I pulled out my wallet and took out a twenty rupee note, seeing this, the guy sitting opposite me took out some money as well, and now the guy sitting next to me brought out some money too after seeing us both. While I doubt the authenticity of that piece of paper, if it was true it would help her, if not she still deserves that money for fooling us all. Either way, she wins.

This is how peer pressure works, you are compelled to do something that others around you are doing. Never wilfully give in to this.

While coming back home I decided to continue that experiment from the morning. I was waiting on a sidewalk to cross the road, other people were waiting too. I rushed in while the vehicles were still moving about, seeing me proceed to cross the road another guy started crossing too, and with this, all the people waiting to cross the road followed suit. What we did was wrong, If I had waited for some more time, the traffic signal would have changed and we could have crossed safely without having to disrupt any vehicles. But no, because of one idiot's action (mine), everyone else turned into idiots and did what he did, textbook sheeple.

Often the first person to act is bound to get mimicked, so if you want to manipulate, affect people, or grab their attention- Think fast, Do fast. Most won't even bother to think if you are right or wrong, they will blindly follow you. A slight nudge is all they need. The current situation plays an important role too, so keep that in mind, and act accordingly.

14 Dec 2023

Trust and Expectations are the heaviest burdens you can place on someone. They are hard to carry and easy to put down. But this is only if you know you are carrying them. You mostly can't help it if someone places their expectations on you. But you can more or less control how much of yourself you show to them, indirectly tweaking their expectations of you. This again depends on the perception and mental ability of whoever you are trying to affect.

Even with all of this, you cannot completely control how others view you, but there is one person who you can take full control of- You.

Expectations are not bad to have, but don't be disappointed if they are not met, because they are your expectations, you set them. If you can't help but be disappointed then don't have expectations in the first place. If you have zero expectations, any slight positive result will exceed your expectations, if not, well.. the outcome is still in line with your expectations.

Think from the perspective of the person you have expectations of. How are they supposed to know of your expectations? How would they know if you imagined them to be something that they in reality are not?

These unrealistic expectations are a result of your flawed perception, your bias, and the creative ability of your mind. If these expectations are not met, who do think you should blame? This is why most relationships go up in smoke when they are formed on the basis of unrealistic expectations, and when these expectations are not met, the people involved feel disappointed and cheated. Don't pin the shortcomings of your brain on someone else.

When I was in school, I didn't overthink much, I didn't know causality, and I wasn't considerate enough to consider others' perspectives, that is why my teachers' expectations of me are justified. But now, I take care not to let people who can impact my life have high expectations of me. It's better to let people underestimate you and be surprised when you exceed their expectations than to let them overestimate you and be disappointed as a result.

I don't care much about others' perceptions or expectations of me, but when the people who can affect your life form high or unrealistic expectations of you, it will end up being troublesome later, I don't want any hassle then, so I'm tying up all the loose ends I can find now.

This is just one way of looking at life, my way. I already told you in the beginning that whatever I say will be biased, so even if it seems convincing, think again. When I narrate a story about me, I will seem right, that is very logical. But you aren't me, are you? Maybe you could be similar to me, but you will never be me. Then, why will the things that worked for me, work for you? There are plenty of other paths to take, explore them, pioneer your own, and make your life yours.

I remembered something else from school, a friend. I never forgot about him to begin with. In grade 8, a new kid joined our class. His name was Vinoth, he wore thick spectacles, and his breath stank. Our teachers got him to sit on the first bench owing to his poor eyesight, guess who else sat on the first bench? This arrangement was so that he could copy down the class notes from me, the funny part of this affair was that I myself couldn't see the blackboard clearly and at times had to copy notes from the ones beside me.

Anyway, we found common ground in PC games after a couple of conversations. He always had a smile on his face and got into fights with almost everyone. His smile hid everything about him. It hid the fact that he had lost both his parents in an accident, and he was suffering from some health issues too. But it wasn't a fake smile put out to conceal his sufferings, it was a smile that only the refugees of true pain could form, it was a smile that warmly welcomed the worst that life could throw at you. It was a smile that challenged destiny asking it what else could go wrong.

And things did go wrong, horribly wrong. During the academic year, he had to go for dialysis every Sunday because of his failing kidneys. After one Sunday he didn't show up at school. His dialysis frequency had to be upped, so he couldn't come to school anymore. There was another friend who lived near his home, so we got his updates through this friend. Even after not attending school for a long time, Vinoth showed up at a couple of our school's events to meet us, his smile was still intact. I kept asking the guy who stayed near Vinoth's home for updates every now and then. During one such exchange, he told me Vinoth wanted PC games, I asked him to take me to his home on the weekend, but he forgot, and I didn't pursue the matter further. I obtained Vinoth's WhatsApp number, we often chatted online.

Summer vacations came and went, we moved on to grade 9. Vinoth barely responded to the messages I sent him. One day I randomly inquired about Vinoth from the guy who lived near his home, he said Vinoth had died during the vacation.

I remembered him smiling, his was a smile that greeted death at his doorstep when it came to fetch him.

15 Dec 2023

Vinoth's dream and life's ambition was to become a boxer, and he believed he could be one. His punches surely packed a good amount of power, I knew this for a fact because that's how he antagonized most boys in our class, by punching them.

His demise was a shock to all of us, he had died months ago and none of us had the slightest clue. The guy who knew about his death didn't tell us till I asked him for an update. He was not at fault here because he did not care enough, but I did, I should have asked about him sooner.

He had asked me one thing, and It was well within my power to fulfill that, but I didn't. I regretted it for a while, but I soon made peace with it. I could do nothing to change what happened, so what good would beating myself up over it do? Nothing.

Since then, I haven't had any regrets. I wouldn't mind if I died right now. You for one, wouldn't get to read this, but since you know nothing about this book now, it wouldn't matter either way. While I would have died without any achievements to speak of, I would still have gone out doing what I wanted to, I was on a path I chose, so it would be a good death, like his.

Having regrets equates to you not accepting yourself. They are the result of either your actions or inaction, put simply- the result of a choice you made. You are a culmination of your choices. By not accepting a choice you made, you are rejecting a part of yourself. If you are fine with that, you are free to have regrets.

Instead of drowning in regret, a better plan of action would be to try and do whatever is possible to lead a life without repeating your previous mistakes.

In the 2nd year of PUC, I started watching anime, it was both a good and bad decision. Good because it was an exciting new world, an almost endless world. Bad because it is very addictive, an indestructible time leech. I still watch anime, I was watching it a couple of days ago too. The majority of the spare time I got during engineering was spent watching anime. Anime got me into Manga, then I found Manhua, Manhwa, Light novels, and Web novels. While I have not read many traditional novels since my 2nd PUC, I was reading thousands of pages of English-translated web novels.

In my 4th or 5th semester holidays, I read an action manhwa. After I finished reading it, I had this indescribable feeling of emptiness. I still can't quite describe it. If you wanted a name, you could call it Existential Crisis. It started with me questioning everything about myself, the maximum impact I could make, and how that would affect anything if it had any impact at all. Human life seemed insignificant, inconsequential even, when viewed on the grand scale of the universe. What was the purpose of everything? Why did we exist, why should I exist? I wanted a reason, I wanted to know what kept people going.

If you remember, earlier I told you that I played games, and thanks to that I had friends of varying ages across different countries. I asked everyone the same question- "What keeps you going? What makes you wake up and look forward to another day?"

It was a surprise question to them, but they all gave me an answer. One person said they were too busy with life to think of things like this, they simply did what they did every day. Another wanted to prove a point to the world. Someone talked about studying well and pursuing a career. They were all mostly talking about their dreams and goals, they had no time to ponder about their existence. There was one person who had had an existential crisis before, they said that it was a phase of life, and it would soon pass. I asked for an answer to my question, they said they didn't know and did not care either.

One thing became clear to me from this whole exchange, knowing or not knowing the answer to this question made zero difference. If I didn't have the answer, I would find it, that would be my driving force, the thing that would keep me going.

As my friend said, it ended soon, or should I say things had just got started. The existential crisis phase ended soon after I had this realization- I knew nothing, but that was still something. It was not always about having all the answers, it was about finding them.

Of all the things, a simple manhwa did this to me, and an action manhwa at that. In that manhwa, the main character is reacting to situations, doing whatever is necessary. Near the final chapters of the manhwa, a character tells him that he never does anything, and that is when it hit me. In a way I was doing what he was doing by being very passive. So when that sentence came flying out of nowhere, I connected to it deeply, tripping into a spiral of endless questions.

16 Dec 2023

If you read that manhwa the chances that it will have the same effect on you as it did on me is as much as me winning the Booker prize. The creator of that manhwa wouldn't have thought that their work could do this to someone. This is the power of art.

Cinema, literature, music, drawings, paintings, all of these have their own soul. Once the creator has done their part, their work becomes a separate entity altogether. Everyone understands and interprets them differently, often in ways the creator could never have imagined or intended for them to be interpreted in.

I have seen people blaming cinema and games for being a bad influence, especially on children. Cinema can only do so much, It is you who decides what you take from it, not the other way around. You should have the basic sensibility to know what to take and what to leave. Since children can't selectively absorb information, there is something called censoring and age rating for movies, even then if they watch something that they shouldn't be watching, whose fault do you think that is?

My headmaster in school used to tell us a thing about blaming others. Whenever you point a finger at someone, remember that three of your own are pointing back at you.

If you want to accuse someone of something, make sure you have more than sufficient evidence to do so. Always have a plan B, but you should never have to use that, that is how thorough your main plan should be.

Even when you want to make a baseless accusation (I don't recommend doing that), be thorough with all the misleading information you can gather, and mix in part truths and rumors. You don't have to prove it, you only have to sell it as the truth. To do that you will only have to plant the seed of doubt. If done successfully, their minds and your deception will work in conjunction. Throughout this process, if you doubt yourself in the slightest, you have failed. The first step is acceptance. You have to accept whatever you have cooked up as the truth, it is no longer a lie, it never was. Fool yourself to fool others.

A significant part of deception and the art of trickery lies in your ability to read a person. Know who you can fool easily, and who you cannot. There is no impossible target, it's just like how you choose your bait based on what creature you want to trap.

This works both ways, if you manage to outwit someone, there will be someone else who will be able to outwit you. Tread cautiously, but remember that excessive caution will only cause you to slip into the sinkhole of paranoia.

Earlier, I told you that I had this feeling of indescribable emptiness after finishing that manhwa. That void inside me opened up because I threw out what previously occupied me- An intense feeling of revenge, coupled with corrosive hatred that was slowly melting the shackles of anger securely imprisoned within. All of this was directed at just one person.

19 Dec 2023

Things my father did and said irritated me, but I always restrained my anger and didn't speak back. I didn't want to escalate the situation, because I liked my peace more than senseless arguments.

But everything has a breaking point, even my hardened resolve to not get involved in useless affairs. On one Sunday sometime during my 5th semester of engineering, a relative visited us along with his son. Seeing me home on a Sunday, he asked me why I hadn't gone out, I told him I had no reason to be out and roaming. Then he started telling me I should be spending the time of my youth outside, roaming around in the city, and not cooped up inside my home.

I ignored him like most companies ignore your engineering grades. But my father decided to join in on the lecturing session. He agreed with what the relative had said and told him how I never go out, and sit in some corner of the home instead. He then told him that ever since I had come home from college the previous day, I hadn't even stepped outside the door. That was it. That very morning I had gone out to buy chicken, and he was the one who told me to get it.

Forget about that day. Why do you think I spent most of my time indoors and not out? Because he was the one who didn't allow me to go out much. According to him, I wouldn't study if I went out and played. All these years of solitude have made me grow accustomed to its company, in solitude was where I was least alone. Now forcing me away from it won't work, because I see nothing that offers a greater value to me, if I did, I would gladly seek it. He was blaming me for the way he shaped me, such twisted logic. On top of that, he was blatantly lying, accusing me of not having stepped out ever since I returned home from college.

I immediately snapped back with "Did your grandfather go get chicken this morning?" He was stunned into silence, and so was that trouble-stirring relative. From that day I didn't speak to him for more than two years. Even after that I only spoke to him because he made an effort to speak to me, and that was at my cousin's wedding. Throughout this duration, my mom tried to make me talk to him, but I refused saying I wasn't at fault. She had to suffer by being a medium of communication between us. This was why I avoided speaking back to the face of nonsensicality because it affected my peace by tormenting my mom.

I wanted revenge against him for ruining everything for me. I wanted to give back to him manifold whatever he had given to me. But sometime down that path I realized that the path I was walking would sooner or later end, and when that happened, that would be my end too. After exacting that revenge there would be no meaning to my life, I would be left stranded in reality. This realization and that manhwa, all happened parallelly. Thus that empty feeling, the feeling of casting away all that which weighted me down.

I would still pursue revenge, but that wouldn't be what drives me, the purpose of my life. That would be a sad excuse for a life. This doesn't mean my father is in my good books, parts of him I acknowledge, some parts I forgive, but I haven't forgotten anything. Never will (unless I live long enough to get Alzheimer's or meet with an amnesia-inducing accident).

20 Dec 2023

At the end of 2019, there was an outbreak of a virus called COVID-19. Early 2020 was when it spread across the globe wreaking havoc. To mitigate damages and bring order, a country-wide lockdown was announced in March 2020.

Our classes were shifted online, and the semester exam was skipped. We still had to write internal tests and assignments and upload them online. We continued onto the next semester digitally.

During this COVID lockdown, a relative in my father's village died. His death was due to COVID-19, but it did not directly cause it. Many people have died after getting infected with the COVID-19 virus, but this uncle of mine didn't get infected with the virus. He killed himself.

21 Dec 2023

Misinformation was on the rise during the COVID-19 outbreak. With a lot of middle-aged people getting access to the internet being new, the effects were chaotic. They started believing whatever nonsense that came their way on social media. Because of some idiots' Fearmongering tactics to get more engagement, so many lives were disrupted.

Somebody started a rumor that eating chicken causes COVID-19, for the next couple of weeks, many poultry farmers sold off their poultry at dirt-cheap prices, some even gave them away for free. This was the perfect opportunity to buy chicken, but my father too believed all the crap that was floating around, so I'll let you imagine what happened next. He always was paranoid but during this Covid outbreak, he took paranoia to new heights. While talking to relatives he exaggerated the effects of COVID-19, he transformed into a pathologist, explaining to others how COVID-19 worked, and others did the same. They mixed in new bits of misinformation with the little true information they knew and spread it. The NEWS TV channels weren't helping, they used clickbait program names and did some Fearmongering themselves too.

Half of the educated folks were falling prey to this Fearmongering tactics, now think of the uneducated folks, the state of their minds.

This uncle of mine was uneducated, most of the middle-aged and elderly people in his village were the same. During the Covid outbreak, the villagers scared him saying that Covid was very deadly, and if you got affected by it, you will die a very painful death, undergoing unimaginable suffering before you die. His mental constitution was already weak, all of this Fearmongering got to him. He decided to take his life before COVID-19 could.

The saddest part of this entire affair is that if he never knew anything about COVID-19 he would still be very much alive today even if he had gotten infected with it. While multiple people in that village got infected with the virus, not one died because of it. It was due to their healthy living habits and strong immune systems. City dwellers were incomparable to them in terms of healthy living and physical fitness.

This is the power of information. Most people don't even pause to verify the information at hand and perceive it as a fact. Be inquisitive but don't get paranoid, use logic, verified facts, and your mind before you draw any solid conclusions.

This wasn't the only death of my relatives during that period. In October 2020 my grandfather died. He was diabetic, had a fluctuating blood pressure, and suffered from other ailments that had become commonplace at his age. I was happy for him that he had passed away peacefully in his sleep, and in his own home, rather than being confined to a hospital bed, punctured with needles, hooked on IVs.

I didn't feel the slightest tinge of sadness, or shed a single tear for him, it was not because I was inhuman or emotionless. It was because it was time, his time to go, a natural process, a grand conclusion to his life.

I had accepted death a long time ago, it was not because of some incident that had happened in my life. It just transpired naturally. Someday randomly, I just viewed birth and death the same way. What use did crying over dead people have, they are not coming back even if you cried out a river. They left you their memories, that should be the most you can ask from them.

A deathless life has no meaning, life is complete only with death. Death doesn't discriminate, no matter who or where you are it will take you into its embrace. It serves as a constant reminder of the fleeting lives we lead. Why fear, and run from it? However further you manage to run, you will be running straight into its open arms.

Do you know what Ashwatthama's curse was? Immortality- An eternity to repent and suffer. The perfect punishment. Death is absolving, this is why I don't like it when criminals of the highest order are given capital punishment. For all the sufferings they have inflicted, death is too light a sentence. Human rights people might have a completely different opinion on this matter, I respect that, but my take on the matter is different. The punishment should serve as a deadly deterrent, it might be crossing the grounds of humanity, but you are dealing with a criminal here, they are already out of bounds. Their plight should be so gruesome that people should shudder in fear to just think of doing what the criminal did. Make them repent, make them regret being alive, make death a luxury to them.

Now do you see the depth of death? Once you see and accept it for what it truly is, your perception of life will change. But don't ever go seeking death, it will come to you when it is your time, till then live a life worth telling death about.

23 Dec 2023

I liked my grandfather, but not his habit of smoking every day. Back then, I was in grade 2 or 3. From what I knew, cigarettes would slowly kill and would cause cancer too. I didn't like him smoking, so I explained to him the harmful effects of smoking which he already knew, surprisingly he quit, and I didn't ever see him touch a cigarette after that. He was strict, but he was very kind, too kind for his own good.

His story always inspired me, and his life taught me life. Skipping school, he used to play with marbles on the streets, unfortunately for him, his father caught him in the act one day, and a few beatings later he was sitting in his school classroom. Not wanting to go to school, that very night he ran away from his home with the pocket change he had, this was when he was less than 10 years old. A few days later he was some 250 kilometers away from his home, in an alien place, where people spoke an alien tongue. The money he brought from his home didn't even get him across the state, he hitched rides on passing trucks to get to Bangalore. So when he got there he didn't have a single paisa on him. He survived on the prasadam from temples, that was his food. He wandered around during the day, and come night he slept outside shops. A shopkeeper was kind enough to provide him with work and a place to stay.

In less than a year after he got to Bangalore, he started sending money to his parents. He started as a construction laborer, and over the years he rose to become a contractor with 10-15 laborers working under him. He bought land, constructed a home, and got married. He supported many of his relatives financially and helped many settle down. He got his brothers' children here and raised them equal to his own, no, better than his own. Food, education, shelter, they got everything that his children got. When they grew up, he supported his brothers' children more than his own. His son aka my mother's brother studied civil engineering to help his father out in the construction field. But by grandfather always favored his elder brother's son, he gave him more control over his construction business, making him the successor.

My uncle was infuriated, he studied computer programming and landed a software job. He even went to the US, refused a permanent position there, and came back home. Going to the States back then was a great thing, he was among the first in our relatives to do so. People ridiculed him for some of his habits, but he's a genius in his own right. He lost his job during the Covid outbreak, he still hasn't got one now. But he's able to sustain his family, pay for the educational expenses of his son and daughter (education isn't cheap), and still have money for emergencies, he did all this, without taking out a loan from any bank, borrowing money from anyone, or selling anything. That's his level of planning and foresight.

Anyway, back to my grandfather's story. As he grew older, all of his construction business was taken over by his elder brother's son. All of his nieces and nephews were settled, and he was instrumental in that. They rarely visited him. At the time of my mom's marriage, his nephew who had taken over the construction business, started causing trouble. Even after the marriage, he interfered whenever my grandfather wanted to do something to financially aid my mom and dad, telling him that my father would waste away that money.

My grandfather trusted his nephew's words and refrained from helping out. In the later years when my grandfather wanted to help us out, he couldn't, because his financial situation wasn't any better than ours. And at that time, none of the people he helped came back to look at how he was faring. Those ungrateful wretches.

> "*Expecting gratitude in return for your help is as big a mistake as being ungrateful to the person who helped you.*"

This is a translated quote from a Telugu movie called Panjaa. Helping someone out to obtain something in return for your help is not what helping means. You help someone because you want to, not because you want something else in return.

My grandfather didn't expect anything in return for his help, that's because he's a great man. But I have every right to call out those scoundrels who mooched off of him and planted the seeds of discord in his family. They are what they are, and where they are today because of him, their prosperity is the alms he gave them. If he hadn't been so selfless, he would be more than a millionaire, his children wouldn't have had to suffer, and would be living a luxurious life now.

After his death, at his funeral, all these rascals gathered to shed their crocodile tears. When he was alive not one showed their face to him, what use did placing flowers on his dead body have? This is why I dislike funerals, all the people gather around a dead body and pretend to be sad while telling each other how great the deceased person was. If only they interacted with that person more when they were still alive. Once dead, nothing you do toward that empty shell matters.

24 Dec 2023

In my 7th semester, I failed a particular subject, the questions that year were harder than usual. The only students who cleared that exam were either the studious type or the ones who resorted to cheating. Most of my friends cheated, they either used a slip of paper that they had sneaked into the examination hall, a smartwatch (the examiners were incompetent, they didn't even know smartwatches could be used this way), or they copied from the papers of the students sitting in front or behind them. A couple of my friends offered to share their cheat slips, but I declined. Firstly, cheating in exams was against my principles. Moreover, to cheat in this pathetic excuse for an exam would be beyond pathetic, it would be worse than stealing from a person begging from a beggar. My standards are not very high, but they certainly aren't this low, so I wrote what I knew, and I believed I could get a passing grade. Unfortunately, I didn't get a passing grade, I had no luck with revaluations either.

In the 5th semester, there was a subject I knew I would fail because I hadn't written enough to obtain a passing grade, but miraculously I obtained a few extra marks in addition to the passing marks. So it was no surprise when I failed in a subject I was supposed to clear. This subject continued to haunt me even after the end of engineering.

There's a fun incident from when we had online classes. Our Head of the Department (HoD) was in charge of teaching us a subject. His assignments were the worst, he gave us a ton of questions to write, and we had to fill up books with ink and sweat to obtain a few measly marks. His classes were lame too, he just read out from some random notes. He always dragged out his useless classes, one time he was going on for more than three hours (1 hour was the normal class duration). He was simply reading out from some random college's notes that were on the internet, we all had these notes too, so he was simply wasting everyone's time. I had had enough, I wanted some revenge for all the time of ours he had wasted. It was an online class, I had the perfect opportunity. I joined that online class with another account, I named it after a film character and started randomly playing songs. The resulting chaos was so satisfying. Our HoD exploded, he started threatening whoever had raided the class, he said he could trace whoever did that and suspend them. He would supposedly get details from the developers behind that online class software. He said he would complain to the cyber crime officials, and spouted a lot of other funny nonsense. Do you think I would do something like this if I could get caught so easily? Not a chance.

I was not overconfident when I said I wouldn't get caught, I had enough measures in place to keep any run-of-the-mill techie from tracing me, and I knew he didn't have the resources to involve tech wizards who could, and this wasn't a crime big enough for anyone who could trace me to get involved. The odds were overwhelmingly in my favor, a situation that met all of my conditions to act.

This is how you take revenge, zero chance of my victim getting back at me, and I barely invested any resources, just a couple of minutes. The icing on the cake was the subject he was teaching us-Network and Cyber Security. Oh, the Irony!

I only told two friends about this, friends who didn't gossip. We all had a hearty laugh. Contrary to what my acquaintances believe, I love pulling pranks and getting back at people. But I only do it after some boxes are ticked, the moment I chance upon an opportunity I take it. During one summer vacation, I had my sister and another niece of mine sitting on the rooftop with empty plates for more than 30 minutes, I told them my aunt would bring them snacks and they sat waiting diligently. It was the night of April the first, they were so gullible. I pulled some more pranks, and they were all fun and harmless.

It worked for me because I avoided lying, I didn't like lying to anyone. The only time I resorted to using lies was to prank people, and that was very rare. My not wanting to lie had nothing to do with being righteous. I simply had no reason to, people only resort to lying when they are fearful of the truth. Moreover, it is a pain to manage your lies. Lying is one thing, but maintaining that lie is the hard part. You have to keep track of what lies were spouted where, the more you lie, the more you become restricted with your words.

But with the truth, it doesn't matter, you don't have to remember what you said to someone, simply put, it is less of a hassle when you are truthful.

With every lie, your words lose power, keep on spouting lies, and someday your words will have no meaning left to them, they will be soulless. I can't afford to do that to my words, because when I give someone my word, I want it to mean something.

26 Dec 2023

Along with the 8th-semester subjects I wrote the exam for that subject I had failed in my 7th semester. The results came sometime around August 2021, I had cleared all the subjects of the 8th semester, but I hadn't secured enough marks to clear that 7th semester subject. That was the only thing keeping me from graduating.

I had to wait for the duration of an entire semester to attempt that exam again. This meant I had to write that exam in 2022, wait for a couple of months for the result, and only then would I be able to apply for apply for jobs.

Most of my friends joined training institutes in September, this was to learn computer programming languages so that they could get jobs in the IT sector. Barely a handful of students were placed in our college's campus placement, and all of them had landed support jobs, i.e. roles like customer support and Tele-calling. You didn't have to complete a hellish course like engineering to get jobs like that, you could get them just by completing your PUC if you had decent speaking skills.

There was an interview for a technical support role, this was part of our campus placement drive, and we were forced to attend it. If you haven't already looked up what campus placements are, they are job opportunities created by companies for students by directly hiring from their colleges. I attended the interview for this technical support role, there were two rounds, and the questions tested my English and computer knowledge, both were my strong points, so there was no way I wouldn't clear them. In the final round, the interviewer asked me if I was fluent in Hindi. I could read, write, and understand it well, but speaking it was not my forte. That is how I lost that job, and it was a good thing that I did. Although it paid more than what my current job pays me, I wouldn't want to work that job, I find dealing with people bothersome, and if this became my job, I'd be jobless within a week of being hired.

There were very few campus placement opportunities for our branch (it's Electronics if you forgot it by now), and all of them were unrelated to what we studied. They were mostly technical support jobs, there was a single interview for a developer role, and that demanded job experience. Seriously? What are they even doing with their brains? How would you find candidates with job experience in a college where the students were in their final year? Our HoD to this day keeps forwarding job openings to our college group, and not one is a role related to electronics.

College placements are supposed to be for every eligible student, but no, my college had to make money out of this too. They said there would be a placement training program for a couple of months. If we didn't join it, we would not be allowed to take part in the campus placement drive. To join this program we had to cough up some money. We were borderline blackmailed into joining this program, we all wanted jobs, that made for a very attractive lure.

Our prestigious college had a grand placement department befitting its stature, it had two important people in it- One Arrogant lady in her mid-30s, and one pretentious guy in his late 20s. They were the dogs..., sorry, they were the gods we had to worship and beg to get a chance of getting a job. They absolutely loved all the power over us they believed they had, their favorite pastime was tormenting students.

All these placement-related activities happened in the last year of Engineering. This training is the right example to explain everything that is wrong with our system. They taught us how to be pretentious, they told us not to be ourselves, this way you would clear the interviews [Insert facepalm emoji here]. Furthermore, they made us solve basic English and aptitude questions and taught us shortcuts to solve them. They were training us to crack interviews, but what after landing a job? The skills necessary for the actual job, no one taught those. We were told we would be taught skills required for a job, but this is what we got. One trainer was telling us stories from the Panchatantra, and another was telling us how to knock on doors. These imbeciles.

That placement training turned out just like college, a complete waste of time and money.

Our college authorities were huge fans of Pokemon. In Pokemon, to be able to challenge the Elite Four, you need to battle all the gym trainers and obtain their badges. Likewise in our college, to get your final exam hall ticket, you had to get signatures from all your professors, the principal, the librarian, and a bunch of other departments. The placement department was one such department. When we went to get the signature from that lady, she asked me if I had been placed yet, I said no, and that I was applying for interviews. Then she retorted with "You will keep applying for the next two years without getting a job." Just why? That was the first time I had ever spoken to her, and 95% of the students weren't placed yet, I hadn't done anything to stand out or offend her, yet she had chosen me of all people to hurl a curse at. Then I remembered my previous notion that all the people who were supposed to be confined to the chains of a mental asylum were roaming about in my college as its faculty.

I got her signature along with her ...frown? I was not sure if that was a frown, I couldn't make out her expression with her contorted face hiding everything behind a veil of unpleasantness.

The Joke's on her though, In less than a year I attended two interviews and obtained both jobs. The last time I visited my college, both of these placement geniuses were missing, apparently they had left the college. I can't even say "good riddance", because the college and they belonged together.

27 Dec 2023

By early 2022 most of my friends landed jobs. My exam was in February, but my preparation for it was the same as before- zero. I had to get rid of that backlog this time, so I started a day early and tried to study a bit. After the exam was done, the waiting game began. The result was finally announced sometime in April or May, I can't exactly remember when, and neither can I be bothered to check for the exact date.

The duration from this result announcement to the 8th-semester results might not seem like much, but after you finish your education, even a week spent at home is heavily subjected to scrutiny. My father was on the edge, he was constantly telling me about random relatives and his friends' children getting jobs, and the salaries they were being paid. Them getting a job is nice, good for them, but what was it to me? I didn't care about them getting a job, neither did I care about their salaries. If this was supposed to spark a competitive flame in me, it didn't work. If I had to do something, I would do it solely for me, I wouldn't do it to be better than someone else. If anything, I would want to be better than my current self.

If I was to have any peace till the results were announced, I had to get my father off my case, and I found the perfect reason. I told him I would prepare for the UPSC exams, I won't go into details about it, so look it up if you want to know more. But I'll say this one thing- It is one of the toughest government exams in the world. Clearing it would make you eligible for the top civil services posts across the country. I was moderately interested in it at first, so I bought books for it and studied a bit too. Just a couple of months before the exam I realized I had bought books and enrolled for the wrong UPSC exam. The most sought-after post after clearing the UPSC exams was the Indian Administrative Service (IAS), which is what the majority targeted. But the one in my sights was the Indian Forest Service, the preliminary exams were the same for both of them, but the main exams differed. I had lost interest at this point, this mixup of mine being one reason, the other was politics. You had to study so hard to get a civil service post, but in the end, your post would still not get the bare minimum respect it deserved from the politicians. The majority of them were almost illiterate, and the entirety of this bunch's educational qualifications were fake. The very thought of shaking hands with them is repulsive.

While the pass percentage for UPSC is around 0.2% (this is what a quick Google search told me), I was fairly confident in clearing it, and I felt that I could. But too bad, I wasn't interested anymore.

During this period, I met with my friends regularly. Except for me and another guy in our class, everyone else had landed a job. I felt nothing of it, I would get one when I would get one. But friends, they were pitying me, they almost made me feel bad about my situation. Pity your enemies, not your friends, that's the worst you can do to someone in an unfortunate situation.

I thought about my career. What skills did I possess which would prove helpful enough to get me a job? I was good with computers and had a decent hold on my words. I didn't have a degree related to either so I couldn't even qualify for most jobs related to them. I was very interested in Ethical Hacking and cyber security, but from what I learned, you couldn't directly get recruited into that role, and the opportunities for them here were pitiful. So there was no point in doing a course related to it.

What was left was programming and development, I wasn't interested in coding, but I thought I could get into UI/UX design, but to get into that I needed to grasp the basics of web development and become a frontend developer first.

I was in the process of learning it when I got the exam results in 2022. I started playing games again, I hadn't played PC games properly in a while, but the learning process wasn't interrupted. In April I saw a random post by someone on Instagram who was looking for content writers. I contacted them, they gave me an assessment, I cleared it and I landed my first paying freelance gig. The pay was absolutely terrible, it was plain exploitation, but this was all I had. I had obtained this without the need for any educational qualifications, so I couldn't leave it. I ghost-wrote hundreds of articles for them in the span of the next three months.

While the freelance gig was ongoing, I randomly found another hiring post on Instagram. It was from a design studio that needed a creative writer. I applied for it, and after an assessment and an interview, I got selected as an intern. I interned for two months with them, the whole process was online. They taught me basic design and related concepts. They primarily did ads, and graphic designing, and managed social media for other businesses. I wrote copy for them, did market research, and made content calendars. I learned a lot from them. They paid me a stipend of 4 thousand rupees for the first month, and when it was time for them to pay me for the second month, they went radio silent.

My father was pressuring me to leave it the moment he got to know the stipend was 4000 rupees. I ignored it and stayed on. Around the time when the design studio folks went radio silent, I had managed to land a full-time job. A friend had sent me a job opening post for the role of a Content writer, I applied for it, they sent me an assessment, after I completed it, they called me for an interview, I got selected.

I didn't want that 4000 from that design studio, I was thankful for the experience and learning I had gotten from them. I sent them a message thanking them, they didn't reply, maybe they thought I would ask for my money. They weren't a big studio, it was just three people in it. So I had no clue about their operating conditions.

My father wasn't happy with me getting this job either, he wanted me to quit this and get a job in IT. I told him this was the best I could get, thanks to the education he got me.

His nagging decreased because the people he was comparing me with got laid off. The IT people my father was telling me about, knew about, and the ones he compared me with were all working in support roles. I was not too fond of those roles, they paid well, and they were easy to get, but they were too monotonous for me. I didn't want to sit the whole day resolving tickets, filling Excel sheets, or talking to customers about their issues.

I had helped a couple of friends clear the initial rounds of their interviews, they were very basic. These job roles had very little scope in the future, I knew that, and people in the IT sector knew that too, but folks like my father only saw the money they made, and thought every job role in the IT sector was the same.

28 Dec 2023

I wasn't actively job hunting even after obtaining the results, this was because I found my skills lacking and I wanted to skill up. But somehow those jobs found me before I went looking for them, and my skills were enough to get me in. I was skilling up to get a UX designer role, but the universe had other plans, and it steered me toward the path of writing. Even if this hadn't happened, I would never have completely abandoned writing. Whatever the job I found, I would still try to write novels somehow, that was my longtime dream. But getting a full-time writing job was unexpected, thanks to this, my writing skills would get better.

There's this quote from Paulo Coelho's The Alchemist-

> "*And, when you want something, all the universe conspires in helping you to achieve it.*"

I found the same happening to me.

Last September was when I started this job, ever since then I have picked up plenty of new skills, met new people, read new books, and gained a lot of new experiences. While on the job, I evaluated assessments of new applicants for the content writing role, and I interviewed a few candidates too. All of this made me realize one thing, my skills weren't merely enough, they were more than enough to get this role.

Many of the applicants had faked their resumes and used AI tools to do their assessments, and in the interview, they spoke nonsense with a straight face, their confidence was shocking. This is what confidence can do, even when it is misplaced.

Once again we come across cheating, I call it cheating because they got caught, but what if they hadn't gotten caught? What if they got selected instead? Nobody except them would know. I already told you this before, it's a crime only if you get caught, the scope of the crime is left to your sensibility and morality.

Following rules is basic discipline, but most of the world runs beyond them, rules are a limiter placed to keep common people running in the hamster wheel. To the people with power, they are like a small fence in front of a tsunami. Money and/or power can bend rules.

Earlier this year, I read a book called "Shantaram," it is by Gregory David Roberts. It had so much life in it, after reading every few lines, I stopped to mull over what I read. In that book, there are bits about corruption. It talks about how corruption in India is a good kind of corruption when compared to corruption in other parts of the world. People here gave bribes to government officials to get them to do the jobs they were hired to do. If you alone insist on following rules, you will be majorly inconvenienced. Analyze the situation, and adapt to it, but be true to yourself, this is the only way you will come unscathed from it.

There was one more line in Shantaram that stayed with me- "The real trick in life is to want nothing, and to succeed in getting it." It's still running about in my mind, it got ingrained into my very being. It will soon be something that I will want, getting it will for sure be a challenge, maybe even the ultimate goal of my life. But that journey will be worth every single heartbeat.

29 Dec 2023

I didn't want to get started on my office life, but I'll tell you about one bitter incident. I lent a colleague two of my books, and soon they quit the job suddenly. I pinged them requesting to return my books. They said they'll send them in a week, after 10 days I asked again, they asked me where I wanted the books to be sent to, I told them to send them to the office. I asked them again after five days, they said I'll be getting it the next day. 8 days after this, I asked again, but no reply, I pinged them again after a month, still no reply...

I had to beg for what rightfully belonged to me. Of those two books, I wouldn't have minded much about one book, I could easily buy it again, but the other book was a part of a box set, if I wanted to buy it, I would have to buy that entire box set again. When I was in the 6th grade, I read the second book of that trilogy from my uncle's collection, I couldn't find the rest of that series then, I couldn't find it for a long time. Recently I checked for it and found a box set in stock, I immediately bought it, and then this had to happen.

I didn't want to give her those books, I find it hard to lend books for this very reason. But whenever someone expresses their interest in reading and asks me for one of my books, the reader in me goes beyond reason to lend them one. I do this even after knowing that there's a very slim chance of me getting them back.

In school, I used to lend my class notes to others and then forget to whom I lent them. This happened often before exams and some people purposefully exploited this weakness by not returning my books, a couple of times my class notes were stolen too. They thought they could reduce my scores by doing this, but back then reading or not reading from my notes made no difference to my scores, so their plans were flawed to begin with.

In PUC I lent a couple of books to a friend, but I forgot to get them back, and after PUC I didn't make contact with him at all. During engineering, I lent out a couple of books, out of four books, I know where three are, but I forgot to whom I lent the fourth one. But I haven't gotten back those three books either, so all of them are as good as Lost.

I don't understand this weird fetish of borrowing things and not returning them. I consider the books I lent to that colleague stolen. If I had the resources I would have filed a complaint against that colleague with the police. Hold on... maybe I should threaten them saying I'll file a complaint, I don't want to waste any more time on this, but... I'll give it some thought and then decide.

Shame is a major limiter, it controls to a huge extent the things you can do, and modesty limits how shameful you can be. But it is your rationality that defines both of these.

I had lent a friend some money because he said it was an emergency. It had been a few months since then and I hadn't asked it back from him yet. The amount I lent to him was a thousand rupees, not a big enough amount to affect my life, but at the same time, it was not small enough for me to forget about. A mentally sound person with a basic sense of morality would give back what they borrowed without being asked for it. I asked him multiple times, and each time he came up with a different excuse. A couple of months ago he called me, he wanted to buy a phone, a smartwatch, and Bluetooth earbuds, he wanted my recommendations. The gall this guy had..., instead of paying me back, he was planning on buying stuff to indulge in, and just last week he asked me if I wanted a movie ticket, he said he had an extra ticket since someone canceled in the last moment. He had money to spend on random unimportant things but he couldn't get himself to return what he owed. The power of shamelessness- it smothers guilt and sets you on a path of unrestrained self-indulgence.

Being shameless is not all bad either, it can help you navigate some situations, which would otherwise be uncomfortable to deal with. It's about how far you are willing to go.

CHAPTER TWO

The Beginning

That is all I have to say. This is the end of this book, an end to one chapter of my life. Getting a job ended one phase of my life and kickstarted another. This new beginning will provide me with new insights, and help me further my understanding of what I know. I might form new opinions, and discard some old ones. Parts of this book- I might not agree with anymore. I don't know what my future holds, maybe you'll know by now.

I wrote this for you, but it is so filled with selfishness, my selfishness to write. Don't think of this as a gift from me, it's the other way around, you kept me from procrastinating, you kept me writing. I have never been this close to my dreams, the only reason I'm here now, is you. I don't have anything to give you that's worth keeping, keep these words for now, these are all I have.

The reason I wanted to write you this was for you to further your understanding of life and forge your own path. But while writing, I realized that I was doing the very thing that I didn't want to, to influence you with my ramblings. I want you to explore things for yourself and form your own opinions, I don't want you inheriting my biases.

I would be lying if I said I didn't want you to read this, but you not reading this would be for the best. It would probably make for a somewhat decent read when you pick this book up in your 60s or whenever you are retired. You would have your own understanding of life then, with this perspective of mine serving to mildly humor you.

If you are reading this and I'm still around, come find me. You can argue with me about the stuff written in this book that you disagree with. Show me your perspective, make me understand.

Most people have this notion about arguments that I disagree with, they think attacking their opponents with fancy words to prove them wrong is the way to go. You don't have to prove someone wrong to win an argument, you only have to make them see your perspective.

Arguments arise when your beliefs don't align with someone else's. Everyone believes in something or someone, to understand the reason behind why someone is the way they are, you will need to understand their beliefs. For this, you need to be able to see beyond your beliefs. Remember, the truly Blind are the people who can't see beyond their beliefs.

With that said, you can come find me even if you don't have anything to argue about. I have a decent collection of books that you can borrow from, you can keep them all too if you love reading. If I don't have my book collection anymore when you find me, I don't know what I have been doing with my life, don't associate with that me, he's a disgrace.

If you want any help or just need someone to talk to, I hope I'm there.

Until we meet again.

www.ingramcontent.com/pod-product-compliance
Lightning Source LLC
LaVergne TN
LVHW041126150826
845673LV00007B/2195

* 9 7 9 8 8 9 2 3 3 6 6 4 2 *